Testing Times

Commentary of Sūrah Mumtahinah

(The Examined One)

By

Shaykh Mufti Saiful Islām

JKN Publications

First Published in March 2021

ISBN 978-1-909114-73-9

British Library Cataloguing in Publication Data
A catalogue record for this book is available from the British Library.

Publisher's Note:

Every care and attention has been put into the production of this book. If however, you find any errors they are our own, for which we seek Allāh's ﷻ forgiveness and the reader's pardon.

Published by:

JKN Publications
118 Manningham Lane
Bradford
West Yorkshire
BD8 7JF
United Kingdom

t: +44 (0) 1274 308 456 | w: www.jkn.org.uk | e: info@jkn.org.uk

Book Title: Testing Times

Author: Shaykh Mufti Saiful Islām

Printed by Mega Printing in Turkey

"In the Name of Allāh, the Most Beneficent,
the Most Merciful"

Contents

Introduction

All praises are due to our Lord, the Creator of the heavens and the earth. May peace and blessings be upon our beloved Prophet ﷺ the seal of all the prophets, his noble Companions ﷷ and those who follow in his footsteps till the last day. Āmīn!

Sūrah Mumtahinah emphasises the hardships, struggles and trials the Prophet ﷺ and the Companions ﷷ faced due to the oppression the polytheists of Makkah Mukarramah put them through. They were constantly plotting and planning against our beloved Prophet ﷺ and his Companions ﷷ, trying their best to turn them back to disbelief.

They tortured and oppressed the Muslims but the Muslims did not retaliate, so the disbelievers came up with one final idea. They presented a proposal to the Prophet ﷺ that they would worship Allāh ﷻ for a year and in return wanted the Prophet ﷺ to worship their idols for a year. This is when Allāh ﷻ revealed Sūrah Kāfirūn which outright rejects this.

The Muslims went through so much persecution yet still had full conviction in Allāh ﷻ and they never became despondent. This teaches us that we should always have patience and faith in Allāh ﷻ with whatever we are going through in life. I pray the Almighty grants us the success the Prophet ﷺ and his Companions had and keeps us steadfast on dīn. I pray He rewards Muftī Sāhib for all his hard work and efforts and grants him Jannatul Firdaws. Āmīn!

Sister Siddīqa Leena
Oldham
December 2020 / Rabīul-Ākhir 1442

Sūrah Mumtahinah

The distinction between belief and disbelief became even more evident when Allāh ﷻ commanded the believers not to befriend and take as allies those who disbelieve. This referred to those who had driven the believers out of their homes and left no stone unturned in persecuting and torturing them.

The believers should not extend their love and friendship to these same disbelievers who harbour hatred in their hearts for them and who wish to exterminate them in every given opportunity they could muster. A distinction is made between those disbelievers who show enmity to the believers, and those who displayed no spite or hostility towards them; they were allowed to be dealt with kindness and justice.

Up until this sūrah was revealed, the believers had been living with their wives, some of whom who had remained following their polytheistic faith and practices. Now the time had come to make their final choice; if a person wished to remain a believer then they could only be married to a believing man or woman. If a person did not accept faith and was married to a believer then their marriage would become annulled and void. The verse forbidding a believer from marrying a polytheist man or woman was revealed in Madīnah, after the migration.

This meant that those polytheists that had been married from the time when the revelation had descended to the Prophet ﷺ would have spent at least 13 years of their marriage to a believer; if their spouse had converted when the message had initially been proclaimed. Allāh ﷻ through His mercy granted this time as a 'transition period' for the polytheists to witness the beauty of faith in close proximity; i.e. that of being married to a believer. If after this great length of time, their polytheist spouse failed to remain moved by the light of truth then it was time for the believer to move on. Also, the believers could no longer marry disbelieving men or women.

Link to the Previous Sūrah

This sūrah mentions another group of disbelievers; namely the Jewish tribe of Banū Nadhīr, who also proved themselves treacherous which resulted in their expulsion from Madīnah. The connection between this sūrah and the previous sūrah is that, whilst in the previous sūrah, the internal bonds of brotherhood amongst the believers was strengthened as a result of expelling the deceitful tribe of Banū Nadhīr, here the bonds of the believers lay in question as Sayyidunā Hātib ibn Abī Balta'ah ﷺ attempted to expose the Prophet's ﷺ secret to the disbelievers. His name was eventually cleared and the believers once again stood as one solid community showing solidarity and brotherhood, and it was with this spirit that the Prophet ﷺ marched with his Companion's ﷺ to Makkah and conquered the city without any bloodshed.

The previous sūrah is so powerful that its link cannot be mentioned alone without mentioning its virtues due to the substantial reward of reading its verses.

In Sūrah Hashr, Allāh سُبْحَانَهُ وَتَعَالَى mentions some of His attributes:

هُوَ اللّٰهُ الَّذِيْ لَآ اِلٰهَ اِلَّا هُوَ ۚ عٰلِمُ الْغَيْبِ وَالشَّهَادَةِ ۚ هُوَ الرَّحْمٰنُ الرَّحِيْمُ ﴿٢٢﴾ هُوَ اللّٰهُ الَّذِيْ
لَآ اِلٰهَ اِلَّا هُوَ ۚ اَلْمَلِكُ الْقُدُّوْسُ السَّلٰمُ الْمُؤْمِنُ الْمُهَيْمِنُ الْعَزِيْزُ الْجَبَّارُ الْمُتَكَبِّرُ ۗ سُبْحٰنَ اللّٰهِ
عَمَّا يُشْرِكُوْنَ ﴿٢٣﴾ هُوَ اللّٰهُ الْخَالِقُ الْبَارِئُ الْمُصَوِّرُ لَهُ الْاَسْمَآءُ الْحُسْنٰى ۗ يُسَبِّحُ لَهٗ مَا فِي
السَّمٰوٰتِ وَالْاَرْضِ ۚ وَهُوَ الْعَزِيْزُ الْحَكِيْمُ ﴿٢٤﴾

"He is Allāh, there is no god but He. He is the Knower of the unseen and the seen. He is the Most Compassionate, the Most Merciful. He is Allāh besides Whom there is no god. He is the Sovereign, the Most Pure, the Giver of peace, the Giver of security, the Vigilant, the Mighty, the Overpowering, the Glorious. He is Pure from whatever (partners) they ascribe to Him. He is Allāh, the Creator, the Perfect Maker, the Fashioner Who has the most beautiful names. Whatever is in the heavens and the earth glorifies Him. He is the Mighty, the Wise." (59:22-24)

Regarding the virtues of reading these verses, Sayyidunā Ma'qil ibn Yasār رَضِيَ اللّٰهُ عَنْهُ narrates that the Prophet ﷺ said:

"When one recites in the morning, "A'ūzu billahis Samī'il alīm minash Shaytānir Rajīm," and he recites three verses from the end of Sūrah Al-

Hashr, Allāh appoints 70,000 angels to pray for him until the evening. If he dies during that day, he dies a martyr. The same applies if one recites it in the evening." (Tirmidhī)

Subhān-Allāh, the great benefit of reciting these three verses in the morning and evening and reaping the reward of 70,000 angels praying for us is an opportunity that no believer should remain aloof from. Inculcating this practice will take a person less than a few minutes a day but the reward is so phenomenal. We need to instill these daily ma'mūlāt (practices) in our lives if we wish to achieve success and great reward. May Allāh ﷻ grant us the ability to act upon this. Āmīn!

Introduction to Sūrah Mumtahinah

This sūrah consists of two rukūs and thirteen verses. It was revealed in Madīnah Munawwarah. When the Prophet ﷺ migrated to Madīnah, the people of Makkah were relentless in pursuing him which led to the battles of Badr, Uhud and Khandaq. It was after this that the peace treaty of Hudaiybiyah took place which was in the sixth year of hijri (migration).

However, not long after the peace treaty was concluded, the polytheists of Makkah broke it. The Prophet ﷺ felt that swift action was paramount and it was with this intention that he marched out with his men to Makkah Mukarramah. When the Prophet ﷺ wished to march out to a certain location, he would not normally reveal the exact location until they had marched out and were at a great distance, and only then he would reveal the destination. This was due to the fact that during his private gatherings and meetings, the hypocrites would also be present. On this occasion however, the Prophet ﷺ announced that he would be heading towards Hunāin but his first destination was Makkah Mukarramah. It was only after the conquest of Makkah that he went to Hunāin.

Sayyidunā Hātib ibn Abī Balta'ah رضي الله عنه was a Sahābi who, after being informed about the Prophet's ﷺ plan, feared for his family. He was originally from Yemen and had settled in Makkah with his immediate family and had no extended family to seek aid or protection from. With the Prophet ﷺ heading towards Makkah, he felt that there would be inevitable bloodshed and his family would end up getting harmed. He therefore, felt that if he informed the Quraysh that the Prophet ﷺ was heading towards Makkah, the Quraysh in exchange would grant his family protection.

Unlike the other Sahābah رضي الله عنهم, his family did not have any security as they had no blood ties with the Quraysh. Even though his intention was only to ensure that his family was saved from harm, he had gone about it in the wrong manner. He had exposed the Prophet's ﷺ secret and Allāh سبحانه وتعالى revealed the opening verses of this sūrah disapproving of the way he had dealt with this matter and cautioned him of the severity of his action:

يَٰٓأَيُّهَا ٱلَّذِينَ ءَامَنُوا لَا تَتَّخِذُوا عَدُوِّي وَعَدُوَّكُمْ أَوْلِيَآءَ تُلْقُونَ إِلَيْهِم بِٱلْمَوَدَّةِ وَقَدْ كَفَرُوا بِمَا
جَآءَكُم مِّنَ ٱلْحَقِّ يُخْرِجُونَ ٱلرَّسُولَ وَإِيَّاكُمْ ۙ أَن تُؤْمِنُوا بِٱللَّهِ رَبِّكُمْ إِن كُنتُمْ خَرَجْتُمْ
جِهَادًا فِي سَبِيلِي وَٱبْتِغَآءَ مَرْضَاتِي تُسِرُّونَ إِلَيْهِم بِٱلْمَوَدَّةِ وَأَنَا أَعْلَمُ بِمَآ أَخْفَيْتُمْ وَمَآ
أَعْلَنتُمْ ۚ وَمَن يَفْعَلْهُ مِنكُمْ فَقَدْ ضَلَّ سَوَآءَ ٱلسَّبِيلِ ۝

"O you who have īmān (faith)! Do not take My enemy and your enemy as friends, offering your friendship to them when they reject the truth that has come to you. They have driven out the Messenger and yourselves because you believe in Allāh as your Lord. If you emerge to strive in My path and to seek My pleasure (you would not befriend the disbelievers). You secretly show friendship to them when I am Aware of what you conceal and what you reveal. The one who does this from among you has certainly strayed from the straight path." (60:1)

يَٰٓأَيُّهَا ٱلَّذِينَ ءَامَنُوا لَا تَتَّخِذُوا بِطَانَةً مِّن دُونِكُمْ لَا يَأْلُونَكُمْ خَبَالًا وَدُّوا مَا عَنِتُّمْ قَدْ بَدَتِ
ٱلْبَغْضَآءُ مِنْ أَفْوَاهِهِمْ وَمَا تُخْفِي صُدُورُهُمْ أَكْبَرُ ۚ قَدْ بَيَّنَّا لَكُمُ ٱلْآيَاتِ إِن كُنتُمْ
تَعْقِلُونَ ۝

"O you who have īmān! Do not take as confidants those besides your own (Muslims). These people would spare no pains to ruin you. They wish for that which causes you suffering. Enmity has been made clear from their tongues, but what their hearts conceal is far worse. Indeed We have made the āyāt (signs) clear to you if you will (attempt to) understand." (3:118)

Sayyidunā Hātib ibn Abī Balta'ah ﷺ wrote a letter to the Quraysh and gave this letter to a woman by the name of Sāra to hand it over to them on her return to Makkah. She had travelled from Makkah to Madīnah. Upon arrival, the Prophet ﷺ had asked her if she had come with the intention of migrating to Madīnah Munawwarrah. She replied that she had not come with this intention.

The Prophet ﷺ then asked her if she had come as a result of converting to Islām. She also replied in the negative. When the Prophet ﷺ asked her the reason of her travelling to Madīnah Munawwarah, she explained that she had been a singer in Makkah where she would entertain men, but after most of the leaders were killed in the Battle of Badr, she had found herself out of work and destitute. This was her reason for travelling all the way to Madīnah Munawwarah; in order to receive financial assistance.

Despite her background, the Prophet ﷺ felt pity for her. He called members from his own clan and asked them to help her. They all donated generously and she had eventually gathered a large amount to take back with her. Despite the kindness shown by the Prophet ﷺ, she was still willing to behave treacherously by taking the letter of Sayyidunā Hātib ibn Abī Balta'ah ﷺ in exposing the Prophet's ﷺ secret and this is what she had set off to do, had she not been intercepted by the Companions of the Prophet ﷺ.

The letter was addressed to the leaders of Makkah, one of them being Ikrimah ibn Abū Jahl, who was the son of Abū Jahl. His father had been killed in the Battle of Badr. Sayyidunā Hātib ﷺ felt that in doing this favour, the polytheists would show compassion to his family and grant them protection. The woman had set off for Makkah Mukarramah and it was during this time that the verse informing the Prophet ﷺ of the events that had unfolded was revealed.

The Prophet ﷺ called Sayyidunā Ali, Sayyidunā Zubair ibn Awwām and Sayyidunā Miqdād ibn Aswad ﷺ. He spoke to them, informing them about the woman who was carrying the letter which contained information about the Prophet's ﷺ plans. The Prophet ﷺ told them to proceed to a place called Rawdah-Khāk. Here, they intercepted the woman and demanded that she handed over the letter.

At first she denied having any knowledge of the letter, but when she realised that the Companions ﷺ of the Prophet ﷺ were serious and would stop at nothing in getting the letter, she reluctantly handed it over. According to some narrations she had hidden it, braiding it within her hair and according to others, she had hidden the letter in her waistband. This incident is mentioned in the following hadīth:

Sayyidunā Alī ﷺ narrates in more details:

Allāh's Messenger sent me, Zubair and Miqdād ibn Aswad, and all of us were riding horses and said, "Go till you reach Rawdah-Khāk where there is a pagan woman carrying a letter from Hātib ibn Abī Balta'ah to the pagans of Makkah" So we found her riding her camel at the place which Allāh's Messenger had mentioned. We said (to her), "(Give us) the letter." She said, "I have no letter." Then we made her camel kneel down and we searched her, but we found no letter. Then we said, "Allāh's Messenger has not told us a lie, certainly. Take out the letter otherwise we will strip you naked." When she saw that we were determined, she put her hand below her waist belt, for she had tied her cloak round her waist, and she took out the letter, and we brought her to Allāh's Messenger. Then Umar said, "O Allāh's Messenger! (This Hātib) has betrayed Allāh, His Messenger and the believers! Let me cut off his neck!" The Prophet asked Hātib, "What made you do this?" Hātib said, "By Allāh, I did not intend to give up my belief in Allāh and His Messenger but I wanted to have some influence among the (Makkah) people so that through it, Allāh might protect my family and property. There is none of your Companions but has some of his relatives there through whom Allāh protects his family and property." The Prophet said, "He has spoken the truth; do not say to him but good." Sayyidunā Umar said, "He has betrayed Allāh, His Messenger and the faithful believers. Let me cut off his neck!" The Prophet said, "Is he not one of the Badr warriors? Maybe Allāh looked at the Badr warriors and said, 'Do whatever you like as I have granted Paradise to you,' or said, I have forgiven you." On this, tears came out of Sayyidunā Umar's eyes, and he said, "Allāh and His Messenger know better." (Bukhārī)

The Companions had used threatening words in an attempt to scare the woman into giving the letter and this made her comply after initially saying that she had no letter. The Companions of the Prophet then returned back to the Prophet and gave him the letter. After reading it, the Prophet ﷺ called Sayyidunā Hātib ibn Abī Balta'ah رضي الله عنه and asked what had caused him to behave in this manner. He replied that he had only done this on account of the fact that he had family in Makkah Mukarramah, and he feared for their safety as they had no blood ties with the Quraysh in being granted protection.

The Prophet ﷺ felt that he had spoken truthfully and his proof for his character came from the fact that he had also participated in the Battle of Badr. Allāh سبحانه وتعالى had granted special clemency to those that had participated in the Battle of Badr so that even if they were to make mistakes, Allāh سبحانه وتعالى would continue to overlook their faults and misgivings.

Allāh سبحانه وتعالى says that when a person sins, by turning to Him in repentance, He will forgive them but for those who had participated in the Battle of Badr, Allāh سبحانه وتعالى says that whatever sins they may carry out in the future, these too have already been forgiven on account of the glorious position and rank they had achieved in His eyes.

In fact, intentionally disobeying Allāh سبحانه وتعالى and His Messenger ﷺ was so far removed from their character that Allāh سبحانه وتعالى commended them with this highest degree of certainty, in knowing that they would be far off from committing such sin with evil intent.

The Prophet ﷺ prayed to Allāh سبحانه وتعالى to keep his plan of marching to Makkah with his men undisclosed. Allāh سبحانه وتعالى answered his du'ā in exposing the plan of Sayyidunā Hātib ibn Abī Balta'ah ﷺ, hence the Prophet ﷺ was able to rectify the situation before any harm or damage could be done.

Allāh ﷻ is reminding the Muhājirūn (migrants) in this sūrah that the polytheists of Makkah were the very people who had expelled them after they had spent their entire lives in the city of Makkah. They had to leave Makkah Mukarramah only on account of their faith.

We have many enemies, the greatest enemy being Shaytān (devil):

إِنَّ الشَّيْطَٰنَ لَكُمْ عَدُوٌّ فَاتَّخِذُوهُ عَدُوًّا ۚ إِنَّمَا يَدْعُو حِزْبَهُ لِيَكُونُوا مِنْ أَصْحَٰبِ السَّعِيرِ ۞

"Indeed Shaytān is your (open) enemy, so treat him as an enemy. He calls to his party (followers) only so that they become inmates of the Blaze." (35:6)

Our nafs which commands evil is also our enemy. We have the three different types of nafs:

1. Nafs-e-Lawwāmah – the reproaching self
2. Nafs-e-Mutma'innah – the self at peace
3. Nafs-e-Ammārah – the self that commands evil

Then there are those who are our enemies within the believers who show enmity. From the disbelievers there are those who are:

- Musālih - those who are on good terms with the believers i.e. have a peace treaty in place.
- Muhārib - have enmity against Islām and seek to destroy it.

The opening verse in Sūrah Mumtahinah warns the people not to take the polytheists as close allies or friends. The believers had shown them affection and love and guided them towards the truth but these people had disbelieved in what had come from the truth and extradited the Prophet ﷺ. They also persecuted the believers to such an extent that they were compelled to leave. Regarding the type of people who we should befriend and have in our company, the Prophet ﷺ said:

"Solitude is better than being in bad company, and being in good company is better than solitude. Saying what is good is better than silence, and silence is better than saying what is bad." (Bayhaqi)

Sayyidunā Abū Hurairah رضي الله عنه reported that the Prophet ﷺ said:

"A man is upon the religion of his best friend, so let one of you look at whom he befriends." (Tirmidhī)

A person tends to follow their peers and this is where they derive their inspiration from. Near the end of time, the Prophet ﷺ said that a person will keep their friends close and stay far away from their own blood ties, such as their father and this is what we see occurring today.

It is clear that people have an influence impacting our lives, subhān'Allāh, even the animals have the ability to do this. Many of the prophets عليهم السلام, before receiving prophethood were instructed to tend to sheep and goats. In caring for these animals moulded their qualities of patience and humility. Tending to these animals developed their forbearance and compassion and this allowed these qualities to blossom in the noble traits of the prophets.

A shepherd may have to lead his sheep through dangerous pathways, ensuring that his sheep do not get lost or left behind. They must also remain vigilant against animals which may be preying upon them. Furthermore, they need to lead their animals to food and water several times a day which could mean walking for miles. A shepherd needs to be tender in order to deal with any injury or illness which may be inflicted on his sheep, and tough at the same time in frightening off predators which may prey on his sheep. These animals themselves are meek creatures. On the other hand, horses and camels are bold creatures and this is the reason that the Prophet ﷺ said that those who rear and breed horses and camels, are those that tend to have pride in themselves.

The dangers of befriending those who have evil intent becomes clear in the following hadīth where Atā Al-Khurrāsāni reported that Sayyidunā Abdullāh ibn Abbās رضي الله عنه said:

"Ubayy ibn Khalaf and Uqbah ibn Abī Muīt were allies. It was the habit of Uqbah, upon returning from a travel, to invite the nobles of his people

to eat with him. Uqbah used to keep the company of the Messenger of Allāh. He returned one day from one of his travels, made some food and invited the people and the Messenger of Allāh to eat. When the food was placed before the invitees, the Messenger of Allāh said to him, "I will not eat your food until you bear witness that there is no deity except Allāh and I am the Messenger of Allāh." Uqbah said, "I bear witness that there is no deity except Allāh and Muhammad is the Messenger of Allāh," upon which the Messenger of Allāh ate from his food. Ubayy ibn Khalaf was absent on that occasion, but when he was informed about what had happened, he said to Uqbah, "You have renounced the religion of your forefathers?" Uqbah said, "By Allāh I did not. I had a man in my house who refused to eat my food unless I bore witness to him, and I was shamed to let him leave my house without him eating, and so I bore witness to him and he ate my food." Ubayy ibn Khalaf said to him, "I will never be happy with you until you go to him, spit on his face and step on his neck." Uqbah did just that.

It was regarding him that the following verses were revealed:

وَيَوْمَ يَعَضُّ ٱلظَّالِمُ عَلَىٰ يَدَيْهِ يَقُولُ يَٰلَيْتَنِي ٱتَّخَذْتُ مَعَ ٱلرَّسُولِ سَبِيلًا ﴿٢٧﴾
يَٰوَيْلَتَىٰ لَيْتَنِي لَمْ أَتَّخِذْ فُلَانًا خَلِيلًا ﴿٢٨﴾ لَّقَدْ أَضَلَّنِي عَنِ ٱلذِّكْرِ بَعْدَ إِذْ جَآءَنِي ۗ وَكَانَ
ٱلشَّيْطَٰنُ لِلْإِنسَٰنِ خَذُولًا ﴿٢٩﴾

"The day when the oppressor will bite his hands saying, 'If only I had chosen the path with the Messenger. Woe to me! If only I had never taken such a person as a friend. He has certainly deviated me from the reminder (the Qur'ān) after it had come to

me. Shaytān always deserts man.'" (25:27-29)

كَمَثَلِ الشَّيْطٰنِ إِذْ قَالَ لِلْإِنْسَانِ اكْفُرْ فَلَمَّا كَفَرَ قَالَ إِنِّي بَرِيْءٌ مِّنْكَ إِنِّيْٓ أَخَافُ اللّٰهَ رَبَّ الْعٰلَمِيْنَ ﴿١٦﴾ فَكَانَ عَاقِبَتَهُمَآ أَنَّهُمَا فِي النَّارِ خَالِدَيْنِ فِيْهَا ۚ وَذٰلِكَ جَزٰٓؤُا الظّٰلِمِيْنَ ﴿١٧﴾

"Like the example of Shaytān when he says to man, 'Commit disbelief. 'So when man commits disbelief, Shaytān says, 'I have nothing to do with you. Indeed I fear (the punishment of) Allāh, the Lord of the universe.' The plight of the two is that both shall suffer in the Fire forever. This is the punishment of the oppressors." (59:16-17)

Uqbah ibn Abī Muīt was inclined to accepting the truth but as a result of being influenced by his friend, he declined to let it penetrate his heart and therefore rejected the message.

The Powerful Effect of Words

Hakīm ul Ummah Shaykh Ashraf Alī Thānwi ﷺ was once travelling in a train when another gentleman boarded the cabin and sat down next to him. He asked the Shaykh where he lived, to which the Shaykh replied, "Thānabhāwan." The man then asked, "Do you know a man called Maulānā Ashraf Ali Thānwi? He replied, "Yes, this is myself." The man could not believe that this man was who he claimed to be because of his humble dress and appearance, and decided to test him in order to find out if he really was the person whom he claimed to be. So he asked his first question by saying, "Why does Islām forbid a person from keeping a dog, for there are so many benefits in keeping dogs; they are faithful, they can help people and guard against intruders?"

Shaykh Thānwi replied, "They may have all these qualities but they have no affection for their own species. When one dog sees another dog, it will immediately start to bark. This bad habit will transfer itself upon the Muslims and therefore a person is not allowed to keep a dog." In normal situations, a person is not allowed to keep a dog but there is a scope of permissibility if it is for security reasons or when involved in farming.

The man then put forward his next question by saying, "You people do dam (recite verses from the Qur'ān and blow on water) and give it to people to drink, claiming it will cure people, how is this so?" Shaykh Ashraf Alī Thānwi used inappropriate and harsh words upon hearing this. The man became incensed with anger and said, "You are supposed to be a religious man and then you speak like this?"

Shaykh Thānwi replied, "I just answered your question! If me uttering these words can affect you by getting you angry, won't the words of Allāh affect a person?" For example, reciting Sūrah Fātihah has many benefits. It is the best treatment to cure many diseases, a source of enlightenment for its readers, it keeps a person safe from the fear of their enemies, and it helps alleviate poverty.

These are just a few of its blessings. Also reciting Āyatul Kursī safeguards a person from witchcraft and enemies.

In the last few examples given, we see both the harmful and beneficial effects that reciting specific words can have. The words of faith will save us if what we utter with our tongues is equally testified by our hearts, but will be of no benefit if we do not allow it to penetrate our hearts. Also, reciting specific du'ās and verses will be a means of healing and protection saving us from harm and evil. We see the effects words can have, so imagine the effects divine words have in shaping our physical and spiritual wellbeing.

إِن يَثْقَفُوكُمْ يَكُونُوا لَكُمْ أَعْدَاءً وَيَبْسُطُوا إِلَيْكُمْ أَيْدِيَهُمْ وَأَلْسِنَتَهُم بِالسُّوءِ وَوَدُّوا لَوْ تَكْفُرُونَ ۝

"If they (the disbelievers) find you they will be enemies to you and extend their tongues and hands towards you with evil intent. They wish that you were disbelievers (like them)." (60:2)

The disbelievers would always plot to bring destruction to the believers, and all their effort was concerted in reverting the believers back to disbelief. After exhausting all avenues in being spiteful and abusive, they came to the Prophet ﷺ and put the following proposal forward: they would worship Allāh ﷻ for one year and in return, the Prophet ﷺ had to worship their idols for the next year. It was then that the following verses were revealed:

قُلْ يَٰٓأَيُّهَا ٱلْكَٰفِرُونَ ﴿١﴾ لَآ أَعْبُدُ مَا تَعْبُدُونَ ﴿٢﴾ وَلَآ أَنتُمْ عَٰبِدُونَ مَآ أَعْبُدُ ﴿٣﴾ وَلَآ أَنَا۠ عَابِدٌ مَّا عَبَدتُّمْ ﴿٤﴾ وَلَآ أَنتُمْ عَٰبِدُونَ مَآ أَعْبُدُ ﴿٥﴾ لَكُمْ دِينُكُمْ وَلِىَ دِينِ ﴿٦﴾

"Say, 'O disbelievers!' I do not worship what you worship nor do you worship what I worship. I am neither a worshipper of that which you worship, nor are you worshippers of that which I worship. For you is your religion and for me is mine.'" (109:1-6)

In another place Allāh ﷻ addresses the believers by saying:

يَٰٓأَيُّهَا ٱلَّذِينَ ءَامَنُوا۟ ٱدْخُلُوا۟ فِى ٱلسِّلْمِ كَآفَّةً وَلَا تَتَّبِعُوا۟ خُطُوَٰتِ ٱلشَّيْطَٰنِ ۚ إِنَّهُۥ لَكُمْ عَدُوٌّ مُّبِينٌ ﴿﴾

"O you who have īmān! Enter into Islām completely and do not follow in the footsteps of Shaytān, for he is certainly your open enemy." (2:208)

As believers it is imperative that we enter into Islām fully, without neglecting any aspects of dīn. For example, there are those who will only pray the Jumu'ah prayers whilst the rest of the five daily prayers are neglected. One sister came to the Shaykh complaining about her husband, by saying that although he fasted in the month of Ramadhān, he only prayed the Jumu'ah prayer and apart from this prayer, she had never seen him pray any other salāh.

Every Man for Himself

لَن تَنفَعَكُمْ أَرْحَامُكُمْ وَلَآ أَوْلَادُكُمْ ۚ يَوْمَ الْقِيٰمَةِ يَفْصِلُ بَيْنَكُمْ ۚ وَاللَّهُ بِمَا تَعْمَلُونَ بَصِيرٌ ۝

"Neither your relatives nor your children will help you on the Day of Judgement. You will be separated. Allāh is Watchful over what you do." (60:3)

On the day when the trumpet will be blown, all links of genealogy will be severed. On that day, everyone will flee from one another on account of the fear that will grasp them. It will be announced:

وَامْتَازُوا الْيَوْمَ أَيُّهَا الْمُجْرِمُونَ ۝

"Separate yourselves today, O you criminals." (36:59)

Once Imām Abū Hanīfah ﵀ recited this verse in his salāh and wept all night until the morning on account of the fear he felt in his heart; fearing that he might be from this category of people. Allāh ﷻ will judge every individual, and those who did not believe will end up in the fire of Jahannam (Hellfire). Those who believed and carried out righteous deeds and actions will be blessed with Jannah (Paradise).

Umar ibn Abdul-Azīz ﵀; although his rule only lasted two years, the Muslims during that time enjoyed so much prosperity that when the zakāh was given door to door, the people would have no need for it.

When he was in his final moments and about to depart from the world, he had no possessions that he owned or even any inheritance to leave behind for his children. The people approached Umar ibn Abdul-Azīz and asked him, “What is going to happen to your children?”

Umar ibn Abdul-Azīz replied, “If they are good, Allāh will look after them and if they are evil, then I do not wish to leave my wealth for my bad children because this will be a curse for me.”

A person’s main concern should be as to whether they are leaving their children in a good state in terms of their piety and taqwa (God consciousness). If we bring our children up teaching them the dīn (religion), then Allāh will cause them to be a blessing for us in the Ākhirah (Hereafter). However, if we fail in teaching the dīn and as a result, they become astray, on the Day of Judgement they will wish to extract retribution from us:

وَقَالَ الَّذِينَ كَفَرُوا رَبَّنَا أَرِنَا الَّذَيْنِ أَضَلَّانَا مِنَ الْجِنِّ وَالْإِنسِ نَجْعَلْهُمَا تَحْتَ أَقْدَامِنَا
لِيَكُونَا مِنَ الْأَسْفَلِينَ ۝

“Those who commit disbelief will say, ‘O our Lord! Show us the two groups from the jinn and humankind who misled us. We want to trample them beneath our feet so that they become of those who are most humiliated.’” (41:29)

Hakīmul Ummah, Shaykh Ashraf Alī Thānwi had mentioned an

incident where some parents had sent their son all the way from India to come to the UK and study. This incident took place about 100 years ago, so one can only imagine the cost involved back then for parents who were from poverty stricken countries. The son, on completing his degree, returned back to India but upon arriving home, he fell seriously ill.

As he reached his last moments, the parents wept and sobbed, saying how they had spent 25,000 rupees (which amounted to a lot of money 100 years ago) on his education, but did not get to see the fruits of their efforts. The son, as he was in his last throes of death could see the angel of punishment visible in front of his eyes and before he breathed his last, he conveyed to them what he was seeing in front of his eyes. He said how his parents had not befriended him, but had rather shown that they were his worst enemies by not teaching him the dīn (religion) and as a result he died in a state of disobedience. May Allāh protect us all from such fate!

فَإِذَا جَآءَتِ ٱلصَّآخَّةُ ﴿٣٣﴾ يَوْمَ يَفِرُّ ٱلْمَرْءُ مِنْ أَخِيهِ ﴿٣٤﴾ وَأُمِّهِۦ وَأَبِيهِ ﴿٣٥﴾
وَصَٰحِبَتِهِۦ وَبَنِيهِ ﴿٣٦﴾ لِكُلِّ ٱمْرِئٍ مِّنْهُمْ يَوْمَئِذٍ شَأْنٌ يُغْنِيهِ ﴿٣٧﴾

"So when the deafening scream will come, on that day man will run from his brother, his mother, his father, his wife and his sons. On that day, every one of them will be preoccupied with a predicament that will make him oblivious of another." (80:33-37)

The situation will be so severe you'd see people drowning in their own sweat. The Prophet ﷺ said:

"The sun will come close to the creation on the Day of Judgement until it will be like one mile from them. People will then drown to the extent of their actions. From among them, there will be those who will be in their sweat up to their ankles. Others will be up to their knees. Some will be in sweat up to their waist, and others will be in sweat up to their mouths." (Muslim)

وَاتَّقُوا يَوْمًا لَّا تَجْزِي نَفْسٌ عَن نَّفْسٍ شَيْئًا وَلَا يُقْبَلُ مِنْهَا شَفَاعَةٌ وَلَا يُؤْخَذُ مِنْهَا عَدْلٌ
وَلَا هُمْ يُنصَرُونَ ۝

"Fear the Day (of Judgement) when one soul will not pay anything towards another, no intercession will be accepted, no ransom will be taken, and they (the disbelievers) will not be helped." (2:48)

Example of Sayyidunā Ibrāhīm عليه السلام

قَدْ كَانَتْ لَكُمْ أُسْوَةٌ حَسَنَةٌ فِي إِبْرَاهِيمَ وَالَّذِينَ مَعَهُ إِذْ قَالُوا لِقَوْمِهِمْ إِنَّا بُرَآؤُا مِنكُمْ وَمِمَّا
تَعْبُدُونَ مِن دُونِ اللَّهِ كَفَرْنَا بِكُمْ وَبَدَا بَيْنَنَا وَبَيْنَكُمُ الْعَدَاوَةُ وَالْبَغْضَاءُ أَبَدًا حَتَّىٰ
تُؤْمِنُوا بِاللَّهِ وَحْدَهُ إِلَّا قَوْلَ إِبْرَاهِيمَ لِأَبِيهِ لَأَسْتَغْفِرَنَّ لَكَ وَمَا أَمْلِكُ لَكَ مِنَ اللَّهِ مِن شَيْءٍ ۖ
رَّبَّنَا عَلَيْكَ تَوَكَّلْنَا وَإِلَيْكَ أَنَبْنَا وَإِلَيْكَ الْمَصِيرُ ۝

"There was certainly an excellent example for you in Ibrāhīm and those who followed him when they said to their people, 'We absolve ourselves from you and from that which you worship apart from Allāh. We reject you (your beliefs). Enmity and hatred have surfaced between yourselves and us forever until you believe in one Allāh.' Except for the statement of Ibrāhīm to his father when he said, 'I shall definitely pray to Allāh for your forgiveness. I have no power to do anything for you against (the punishment of) Allāh. O our Lord! In You do we trust, to You do we turn and to You shall we return.'" (60:4)

Allāh سبحانه وتعالى gives the example of Sayyidunā Ibrāhīm عليه السلام. His father not only worshipped idols, but he would make these idols for worshipping. When it came to following his father in worshipping idols, Sayyidunā Ibrāhīm عليه السلام refused to obey him. He remained firm and distanced himself from his people. He warned his father about the futility of idol worship:

إِذْ قَالَ لِأَبِيهِ يَٰٓأَبَتِ لِمَ تَعْبُدُ مَا لَا يَسْمَعُ وَلَا يُبْصِرُ وَلَا يُغْنِي عَنكَ شَيْـًٔا ﴿٤٢﴾ يَٰٓأَبَتِ إِنِّي قَدْ
جَآءَنِي مِنَ ٱلْعِلْمِ مَا لَمْ يَأْتِكَ فَٱتَّبِعْنِيٓ أَهْدِكَ صِرَٰطًا سَوِيًّا ﴿٤٣﴾ يَٰٓأَبَتِ لَا تَعْبُدِ ٱلشَّيْطَٰنَ ۖ
إِنَّ ٱلشَّيْطَٰنَ كَانَ لِلرَّحْمَٰنِ عَصِيًّا ﴿٤٤﴾ يَٰٓأَبَتِ إِنِّيٓ أَخَافُ أَن يَمَسَّكَ عَذَابٌ مِّنَ ٱلرَّحْمَٰنِ
فَتَكُونَ لِلشَّيْطَٰنِ وَلِيًّا ﴿٤٥﴾ قَالَ أَرَاغِبٌ أَنتَ عَنْ ءَالِهَتِي يَٰٓإِبْرَٰهِيمُ ۖ لَئِن لَّمْ تَنتَهِ لَأَرْجُمَنَّكَ
وَٱهْجُرْنِي مَلِيًّا ﴿٤٦﴾

"When he told his father, 'O my beloved father! Why do you worship things that cannot hear, cannot see and cannot be of

any assistance to you? O my beloved father! Such knowledge has come to me that has not come to you, so follow me and I shall show you the straight path. O my beloved father! Do not worship Shaytān. Indeed Shaytān was ever disobedient to Ar-Rahmān (the Most Merciful). O my beloved father! Indeed I fear that a punishment would afflict you from Ar-Rahmān, after which you would be a friend of Shaytān.' His father retorted, 'Do you dislike my gods, O Ibrāhīm? If you do not stop, I shall surely stone you. (It is best that you) leave me forever.'" (19:42-46)

After hearing his father's response, he responded to his father:

قَالَ سَلَٰمٌ عَلَيۡكَۖ سَأَسۡتَغۡفِرُ لَكَ رَبِّيٓۖ إِنَّهُۥ كَانَ بِي حَفِيّٗا ﴿٤٧﴾ وَأَعۡتَزِلُكُمۡ وَمَا تَدۡعُونَ مِن
دُونِ ٱللَّهِ وَأَدۡعُواْ رَبِّي عَسَىٰٓ أَلَّآ أَكُونَ بِدُعَآءِ رَبِّي شَقِيّٗا ﴿٤٨﴾

"Ibrāhīm said, 'Peace be on you. I shall shortly seek forgiveness from my Lord on your behalf. He has always been compassionate towards me. I shall separate myself from you and from that which you worship instead of Allāh. Then I shall call to my Lord. I am hopeful that I shall not be deprived in my call to my Lord.'" (19:47-48)

Sayyidunā Ibrāhīm عليه السلام still hoped that his father would go on to embrace Islām but this did not come to be. For a person to be guided, they must seek guidance at least or hope to be guided rightly but Sayyidunā Ibrāhīm's عليه السلام father had closed every avenue of the mercy of his Lord from reaching him. As a result of this, he died as a disbeliever.

Our love and hatred for a person should also be for the sake of pleasing Allāh ﷻ and not for our own personal reasons. The best of all good deeds is to have love and hatred for the sake of Allāh ﷻ as mentioned in the following hadīth:

Sayyidunā Abū Umāmah ؓ reported that the Messenger of Allāh ﷺ said:

"Whoever loves for the sake of Allāh, hates for the sake of Allāh, gives for the sake of Allāh and withholds for the sake of Allāh has perfected their faith." (Abū Dāwūd)

There will be seven categories of people who will be under the shade of Allāh's ﷻ throne on the Day of Judgement. One of these categories will be those two people who loved each other for the sake of Allāh ﷻ. They would gather for the sake of Allāh ﷻ and part for the sake of Allāh. Even the Prophets ﷺ and the Sahābah will be astonished at their positions. The Messenger of Allāh ﷺ said:

Allāh has said, "For those who love each other for the sake of My glory, they will be given thrones of light; and the prophets and martyrs will be envious of them." (Tirmidhī)

This does not mean that these people will have a higher position than the prophets and the martyrs but rather, the hadīth highlights the superior position that they will reach as a result of the love and compassion they had for one another. It will reach the extent, that even the prophets and martyrs will marvel at the reward granted to them.

Allāh سبحانه وتعالى praises Sayyidunā Ibrāhīm عليه السلام so much, and in one particular instance, Sayyidunā Ibrāhīm عليه السلام makes du'ā to Allāh سبحانه وتعالى to be remembered by the generations that would come:

وَاجْعَل لِّي لِسَانَ صِدْقٍ فِي الْآخِرِينَ ﴿٨٤﴾ وَاجْعَلْنِي مِن وَرَثَةِ جَنَّةِ النَّعِيمِ ﴿٨٥﴾

"Maintain a favourable word for me among those who are to come. And make me from the inheritors of the bounteous Jannah." (26: 84-85)

Allāh سبحانه وتعالى accepted this du'ā. Out of all the prophets, Sayyidunā Ibrāhīm عليه السلام is mentioned abundantly in the Qur'an and ahādīth. Furthermore, followers of all religions respect and honour him. For example, when we pray our salāh, we read Durūd-e-Ibrāhīm:

"O Allāh shower Your blessings on Muhammad and his family as You showered Your mercy on Ibrāhīm and his family. Surely You are Praiseworthy and Glorious. O Allāh bless Muhammad and his family as You blessed Ibrāhīm and his family. Surely, You are Praiseworthy and Glorious."

From this, we can understand that it is a praiseworthy act to leave something behind as sadaqah jāriyah (ongoing charity), for example through building a well, helping towards building a masjid or a madrasah, leaving behind pious children who make du'ā for us or writing a book; in leaving knowledge behind.

We make the du'ā prescribed in the Qur'ān when Allāh سبحانه وتعالى mentions the qualities of the I'bādur Rahmān (servants of the Merciful):

وَالَّذِينَ يَقُولُونَ رَبَّنَا هَبْ لَنَا مِنْ أَزْوَاجِنَا وَذُرِّيّٰتِنَا قُرَّةَ أَعْيُنٍ وَّاجْعَلْنَا لِلْمُتَّقِينَ إِمَامًا ۝

"Those who say, 'O our Lord! Grant us the coolness of our eyes from our spouses and children and make us imāms (guides) of the pious." (25:74)

وَمَا كَانَ اسْتِغْفَارُ إِبْرٰهِيمَ لِأَبِيهِ إِلَّا عَنْ مَّوْعِدَةٍ وَّعَدَهَا إِيَّاهُ فَلَمَّا تَبَيَّنَ لَهُ أَنَّهُ عَدُوٌّ لِّلّٰهِ تَبَرَّأَ مِنْهُ ۚ إِنَّ إِبْرٰهِيمَ لَأَوَّاهٌ حَلِيمٌ ۝

"Ibrāhīm sought forgiveness for his father only because of a promise that he had made to him. When it became clear to him that his father was Allāh 's enemy he absolved himself from him. Indeed Ibrāhīm was extremely soft-hearted and tolerant." (9:114)

Our reliance should always be upon Allāh سبحانه وتعالى. A person will only be guided if they wish to be guided, but they have to take the first step in seeking guidance.

أَنُلْزِمُكُمُوهَا وَأَنْتُمْ لَهَا كٰرِهُونَ ۝

"Can we force it on to you when you disapprove of it?" (11:28)

The Prophet ﷺ showed us the path of guidance but the ultimate choice lies with us in making our decision.

مَا كَانَ لِلنَّبِيِّ وَالَّذِينَ آمَنُوٓا أَن يَسْتَغْفِرُوا لِلْمُشْرِكِينَ وَلَوْ كَانُوٓا أُو۟لِي قُرْبَىٰ مِنۢ بَعْدِ مَا تَبَيَّنَ لَهُمْ أَنَّهُمْ أَصْحَٰبُ ٱلْجَحِيمِ ۝

"It is not permissible for the Prophet, nor the believers to seek forgiveness for the Mushrikīn (polytheists), even if they be their relatives, after it has become clear to them that they are to be residents of the Blaze." (9:113)

ثُمَّ أَوْحَيْنَآ إِلَيْكَ أَنِ ٱتَّبِعْ مِلَّةَ إِبْرَٰهِيمَ حَنِيفًا ۖ وَمَا كَانَ مِنَ ٱلْمُشْرِكِينَ ۝

"Then We sent revelation to you: 'Follow the religion of Ibrāhīm that is Hanīf (belief in one God). He was not from the Mushrikūn (polytheists).'" (16:123)

Du'ā in a Time of Difficulty

رَبَّنَا لَا تَجْعَلْنَا فِتْنَةً لِّلَّذِينَ كَفَرُوا وَٱغْفِرْ لَنَا رَبَّنَآ ۖ إِنَّكَ أَنتَ ٱلْعَزِيزُ ٱلْحَكِيمُ ۝

"O our Lord! Do not make us a test for the disbelievers and forgive (us). O our Lord, Indeed You are the Mighty, the Wise." (60:5)

This du'ā should be made for all the Muslims who are suffering across the globe. At times we may be tested through suffering and hardship at the hands of the disbelievers. At other times, the believers may suffer from so much fitnah (trials and tribulations) that the disbelievers will keep themselves far away from the Muslims in thinking that the religion of Islām is a source of evil.

Everything Praises Allāh ﷻ

لَقَدْ كَانَ لَكُمْ فِيهِمْ أُسْوَةٌ حَسَنَةٌ لِّمَن كَانَ يَرْجُو اللَّهَ وَالْيَوْمَ الْآخِرَ ۚ وَمَن يَتَوَلَّ فَإِنَّ اللَّهَ هُوَ الْغَنِيُّ الْحَمِيدُ ۞

"There was certainly an excellent example in them for those of you who believe in Allāh and the Last Day. As for him who turns away, Allāh certainly is Independent, Most worthy of Praise." (60:6)

This verse is referring to the prophet Sayyidunā Ibrāhīm ؑ and his followers. In another verse, Allāh ﷻ says:

لَقَدْ كَانَ لَكُمْ فِي رَسُولِ اللَّهِ أُسْوَةٌ حَسَنَةٌ لِّمَن كَانَ يَرْجُو اللَّهَ وَالْيَوْمَ الْآخِرَ وَذَكَرَ اللَّهَ كَثِيرًا ۞

"There is definitely an excellent example in Allāh's Messenger for the one who fears Allāh and the Last Day and who remembers Allāh abundantly." (33:21)

For those who disbelieve, then the life of this world is all that they can hope for:

وَقَالُوا مَا هِيَ إِلَّا حَيَاتُنَا الدُّنْيَا نَمُوتُ وَنَحْيَا وَمَا يُهْلِكُنَا إِلَّا الدَّهْرُ ۚ وَمَا لَهُم بِذَٰلِكَ مِنْ عِلْمٍ ۖ إِنْ هُمْ إِلَّا يَظُنُّونَ ۝

"They (the disbelievers) say, 'This is nothing but our worldly life. We live and die and it is only time that will destroy us. They have no proof of this but only speculate." (45:24)

In a hadīth qudsī, Allāh ﷻ says:

"O My servants, if the first and the last of you and the human and the jinn of you were as pious as the most pious heart of anyone among you, it would not add anything to My dominion. O My servants, if the first and the last of you and the human and the jinn of you were as wicked as the most wicked of anyone among you, it would not decrease anything of My dominion." (Muslim)

He is Al-Hamīd – the One Who is praised by all of creation. Allāh ﷻ says:

يُسَبِّحُ لِلَّهِ مَا فِي السَّمَاوَاتِ وَمَا فِي الْأَرْضِ ۖ لَهُ الْمُلْكُ وَلَهُ الْحَمْدُ ۖ وَهُوَ عَلَىٰ كُلِّ شَيْءٍ قَدِيرٌ ۝

"Whatever is in the heavens and on earth glorify Allāh. All kingdom and all praise belong to Him and He has power of all things." (64:1)

سَبَّحَ لِلَّهِ مَا فِي السَّمَاوَاتِ وَمَا فِي الْأَرْضِ ۖ وَهُوَ الْعَزِيزُ الْحَكِيمُ ۝

"Whatever is in the heavens and whatever is on earth glorifies Allāh. He is the Mighty, the Wise." (59:1)

In the two verses mentioned above, the past, present and future tense is referred to, meaning that Allāh ﷻ was praised and glorified in the past, is continuously being praised and glorified at present and this glorification and praise will perpetuate for eternity.

عَسَى اللّٰهُ أَنْ يَّجْعَلَ بَيْنَكُمْ وَبَيْنَ الَّذِيْنَ عَادَيْتُمْ مِّنْهُمْ مَّوَدَّةً ۚ وَاللّٰهُ قَدِيْرٌ ۚ وَاللّٰهُ غَفُوْرٌ رَّحِيْمٌ ۞

"Allāh shall soon create love between you and those who are your enemies. Allāh is Most Capable and Allāh is Most Forgiving, Most Merciful." (60:7)

After the peace treaty of Hudaybiyah in the sixth year of Hijri (migration), the conquest of Makkah followed two years later. The arch enemy of Islām, Abū Sufyān, who spearheaded all the battles against the Prophet ﷺ and was one of their main leaders; after the conquest of Makkah, he accepted Islām and became from among the Companions of the Prophet ﷺ. Allāh ﷻ is saying in this verse that these people who had so much enmity towards the believers and the Prophet ﷺ will embrace Islām and this deep hatred; by the will of Allāh ﷻ was transformed into love.

In a similar manner Suhāil ibn Amr also accepted Islām. He had been on the opposition side when the peace treaty had been negotiated and when the words 'Muhammad the Messenger of Allāh agrees with Suhāil ibn Amr had been written, he immediately refused to accept this title. He proclaimed that if he had believed Muhammad to be the Messenger of Allāh, then they would not have fought him in the first place.

The Prophet realising the importance of the peace treaty asked Sayyidunā Alī to erase the part mentioning that he was the Prophet of Allāh, but Sayyidunā Alī refused to do this as he felt it was the greatest insult to the Prophet. The Prophet then asked Sayyidunā Alī to point out the words to him which read 'Messenger of Allāh' and he himself erased these words.

Other staunch enemies who, after the conquest of Makkah embraced Islām and became devout believers included: Hakīm Ibn Hizām, Amr ibn Al-Ās, Khalīd ibn Walīd to name a few.

In another place Allāh mentions:

وَاعْتَصِمُوا بِحَبْلِ اللَّهِ جَمِيعًا وَلَا تَفَرَّقُوا ۚ وَاذْكُرُوا نِعْمَتَ اللَّهِ عَلَيْكُمْ إِذْ كُنتُمْ أَعْدَاءً فَأَلَّفَ
بَيْنَ قُلُوبِكُمْ فَأَصْبَحْتُم بِنِعْمَتِهِ إِخْوَانًا وَكُنتُمْ عَلَىٰ شَفَا حُفْرَةٍ مِّنَ النَّارِ فَأَنقَذَكُم مِّنْهَا ۗ
كَذَٰلِكَ يُبَيِّنُ اللَّهُ لَكُمْ آيَاتِهِ لَعَلَّكُمْ تَهْتَدُونَ ۝

"Hold fast to the rope of Allāh all of you together, and do not separate. Recall Allāh's favour to you when you were enemies and He created love between your hearts. Then you became brothers by His grace. You were on the edge of an abyss (pit) of

fire (Jahannam) and He rescued you from it. In this way, Allāh does explain his āyāt (verses) to you so that you may be guided." (3:103)

وَلَا تَسْتَوِي الْحَسَنَةُ وَلَا السَّيِّئَةُ ۚ ادْفَعْ بِالَّتِي هِيَ أَحْسَنُ فَإِذَا الَّذِي بَيْنَكَ وَبَيْنَهُ عَدَاوَةٌ كَأَنَّهُ وَلِيٌّ حَمِيمٌ ﴿٣٤﴾ وَمَا يُلَقَّاهَا إِلَّا الَّذِينَ صَبَرُوا وَمَا يُلَقَّاهَا إِلَّا ذُو حَظٍّ عَظِيمٍ ﴿٣٥﴾

"Good and evil cannot be equal. Resist with that which is best, and the one between yourself and whom there was enmity will instantly become like your bosom friend. Only the patient ones will be inspired with (doing) this. Only the most fortunate will be inspired with this." (41:34-35)

يَا أَيُّهَا الَّذِينَ آمَنُوا كُونُوا قَوَّامِينَ لِلَّهِ شُهَدَاءَ بِالْقِسْطِ ۖ وَلَا يَجْرِمَنَّكُمْ شَنَآنُ قَوْمٍ عَلَىٰ أَلَّا تَعْدِلُوا ۚ اعْدِلُوا هُوَ أَقْرَبُ لِلتَّقْوَىٰ ۖ وَاتَّقُوا اللَّهَ ۚ إِنَّ اللَّهَ خَبِيرٌ بِمَا تَعْمَلُونَ ۞

"O you who have īmān! Stand upright for Allāh bearing testimony with justice. Let not (your) hatred for a nation provoke you to be unjust. Be just! It is closer to taqwā. Fear Allāh! Indeed Allāh is informed of what you do." (5:8)

The treaty of Hudaybiyah was negotiated after the Prophet ﷺ had a dream of himself and the believers going to perform umrah. After seeing this vision, he had set off with 1400 Sahābah ﷺ intending to perform umrah.

Even if a person was to spend all the money in the world, they would not be able to create love between people who had this level of enmity, but Allāh ﷻ showed that this is achievable when a person has īmān (faith).

Also, if a person has enmity for a person who disbelieves, even then they should never exceed the limits. This applies to other cases also. Unfortunately, we see when marriages break down, spouses express such sourness and hate towards each other. This should not be the case. How does the Qur'ān teach us to act during this situation?

﴿وَلَا تَنسَوُا الْفَضْلَ بَيْنَكُمْ﴾

"Do not forget kindness among yourselves." (2:237)

When a marriage falls apart, then only bitter memories remain, to the extent that even the good times are remembered with an evil twist. By reminiscing over the memorable times, this will help aid the healing process of moving on. Over here we are reminded that even when a marriage is ending, the husband is to deal with kindness to the wife in recollecting the good times they once shared before parting. This will inevitably aid the healing process and help a person in recovering from their loss.

Sayyidunā Anas ibn Mālik رضي الله عنه reported that the Prophet ﷺ said to him:

"O my son, if you are able every morning and evening to remove any rancour from your heart towards anyone, then do so." Then the Prophet said to me, "O my son, that is my Sunnah. Whoever revives my Sunnah

has loved me, and whoever loves me will be with me in Paradise." (Tirmidhī)

Our love and hate should be that of moderation. A person may love someone so much, which is often the case in the initial stages of a marriage but when this marriage breaks down, the depth of hatred that is unleashed has no limits. Similarly, a person may feel hatred towards an individual which may cause them to leave no stone unturned in venting their feelings of hatred. Yet a time may come when this person becomes dear to them and then they are left with regret and remorse at the way they had mistreated that very same person. Many of those who had so much hatred for the Prophet ﷺ initially became so close to him and progressed to make great achievements on becoming the standard-bearers of Islām.

﴿ وَاللَّهُ غَفُورٌ رَّحِيمٌ ﴾

"And Allāh is Most Forgiving, Most Merciful." (60:7)

Here, Allāh ﷻ is saying that even though a person had enmity and they exceeded the limits, Allāh ﷻ is still 'Most Forgiving, Most Merciful.' Hence if a person turns to Allāh ﷻ and makes sincere repentance, then Allāh ﷻ will forgive them and overlook their misdeeds. Sayyidunā Amr ibn Al-Ās رضي الله عنه became the conqueror of Egypt and Sayyidunā Khālid ibn Walīd رضي الله عنه became one of the greatest military commander that the world has ever witnessed.

لَقَدْ صَدَقَ اللّٰهُ رَسُوْلَهُ الرُّؤْيَا بِالْحَقِّ ۚ لَتَدْخُلُنَّ الْمَسْجِدَ الْحَرَامَ إِنْ شَآءَ اللّٰهُ اٰمِنِيْنَ مُحَلِّقِيْنَ رُءُوْسَكُمْ وَمُقَصِّرِيْنَ لَا تَخَافُوْنَ ۖ فَعَلِمَ مَا لَمْ تَعْلَمُوْا فَجَعَلَ مِنْ دُوْنِ ذٰلِكَ فَتْحًا قَرِيْبًا ۞

"Verily, Allāh shall make the dream of His Messenger come precisely true. When Allāh wills, you shall definitely enter the Masjid Harām in peace with your hair shaved or trimmed without any fear. Allāh had knowledge of that about which you were unaware and has decreed a near victory even before this." (48:27)

Showing Kindness

لَا يَنْهٰكُمُ اللّٰهُ عَنِ الَّذِيْنَ لَمْ يُقَاتِلُوْكُمْ فِي الدِّيْنِ وَلَمْ يُخْرِجُوْكُمْ مِّنْ دِيَارِكُمْ أَنْ تَبَرُّوْهُمْ وَتُقْسِطُوْٓا إِلَيْهِمْ ۖ إِنَّ اللّٰهَ يُحِبُّ الْمُقْسِطِيْنَ ۞

"Allāh does not forbid you from behaving cordially and justly towards those who do not fight you for (reason of your) religion and who do not drive you out from your homes. Verily Allāh loves those who are just." (60:8)

This verse was revealed regarding the mother of Sayyidah Asmā رضي الله عنها, Qutaylah bint Abdul Uzzā. After Sayyidunā Abū Bakr رضي الله عنه embraced Islām, he divorced his first wife. His second wife was Sayyidah

Umme Rūmān ﷺ who was the mother of Sayyidah Ā'ishah ﷺ.

After the Prophet ﷺ and his Companions ﷺ had migrated to Madīnah, Qutaylah came to Madīnah Munawwarah to ask her daughter for assistance. Sayyidah Asmā ﷺ became a little apprehensive as to whether she was allowed to help her, given that she was a polytheist. These were the people who had shown enmity against the Muslims.

Sayyidah Asmā ﷺ asked the Prophet ﷺ, "Can I show kindness to my mother?" The Prophet ﷺ replied, "Yes, show kindness and compassion to your mother."

Within the non-Muslims, there are two categories:

1) Ahl-dhimmah – those who live in an Islamic state or country.

The Prophet ﷺ said:

"Whoever killed a Mu'āhid (a person who is granted the protection by the Muslim state) shall not smell the fragrance of Paradise though its fragrance can be smelled at a distance of 40 years of travelling." (Bukhārī)

Such is the status and rights accorded to non-Muslims who are living under Muslim rule as a citizen of a state or country.

2) Ahlus-sulh – those who are the allies of the Muslims, they are granted the same rights as the Muslims.

Once a rabbi asked a scholar the following question, "In the Qur'ān, it always says negative things about the Jews and Christians."

صِرَاطَ الَّذِينَ أَنْعَمْتَ عَلَيْهِمْ غَيْرِ الْمَغْضُوبِ عَلَيْهِمْ وَلَا الضَّالِّينَ ۞

"And not the path of those with whom You are angry (the Jews), nor the path of those who have gone astray (the Christians)." (1:7)

يَا أَيُّهَا الَّذِينَ آمَنُوا لَا تَتَّخِذُوا الَّذِينَ اتَّخَذُوا دِينَكُمْ هُزُوًا وَلَعِبًا مِنَ الَّذِينَ أُوتُوا الْكِتَابَ مِنْ قَبْلِكُمْ وَالْكُفَّارَ أَوْلِيَاءَ ۚ وَاتَّقُوا اللَّهَ إِنْ كُنْتُمْ مُؤْمِنِينَ ۞

"O you who have īmān. Do not take as friends those who make a mockery and fun of your dīn (religion) from those who have received the Book before you (Jews and Christians) and the (other) Kuffār (disbelievers). Fear Allāh if you are believers." (5:57)

The scholar explained that whilst the Qur'ān criticizes the Jews and Christians for their wrongdoings, it also praises those Jews and Christians who are righteous:

يُؤْمِنُونَ بِاللَّهِ وَالْيَوْمِ الْآخِرِ وَيَأْمُرُونَ بِالْمَعْرُوفِ وَيَنْهَوْنَ عَنِ الْمُنْكَرِ وَيُسَارِعُونَ فِي الْخَيْرَاتِ وَأُولَٰئِكَ مِنَ الصَّالِحِينَ ۞

"They are not alike. From the people of the Book is a group who are upright. They recite the verses of Allāh in the hours of the night and prostrate. They believe in Allāh and the Last Day, they command what is right, forbid evil and hasten to do good deeds. These are from among the righteous ones." (3:114)

وَمِنْ أَهْلِ الْكِتَٰبِ مَنْ إِنْ تَأْمَنْهُ بِقِنْطَارٍ يُؤَدِّهِۦٓ إِلَيْكَ وَمِنْهُمْ مَّنْ إِنْ تَأْمَنْهُ بِدِينَارٍ لَّا يُؤَدِّهِۦٓ
إِلَيْكَ إِلَّا مَا دُمْتَ عَلَيْهِ قَآئِمًا ۗ ذَٰلِكَ بِأَنَّهُمْ قَالُوا۟ لَيْسَ عَلَيْنَا فِى الْأُمِّيِّۦنَ سَبِيلٌ وَيَقُولُونَ عَلَى
اللَّهِ الْكَذِبَ وَهُمْ يَعْلَمُونَ ﴾

"From the People of the Book there is he who, if you trust him with a wealth of treasures, he will return it to you. Then there is he who, if you trust him with a single dīnar (gold coin), he will not return it to you unless you keep standing over him. This is because they say, 'We have no obligation towards the unlettered people.' They lie about Allāh knowingly." (3:75)

﴿ وَإِنَّ مِنْ أَهْلِ الْكِتَٰبِ لَمَنْ يُؤْمِنُ بِاللَّهِ وَمَآ أُنْزِلَ إِلَيْكُمْ وَمَآ أُنْزِلَ إِلَيْهِمْ خَٰشِعِينَ لِلَّهِ ﴾

"Without doubt there are those from the People of the Book who believe in Allāh, in what has been revealed to you and what has been revealed to them, they humble themselves before Allāh" (3:199)

Not only do we have to fulfil the rights and responsibilities of people irrespective of their faith, but even the rights of animals. We must also ensure that animals are not forgotten and that they too are granted the right to kind treatment and of being looked after.

Sayyidunā Abdullāh ibn Umar ﵄ narrated that the Messenger of Allāh ﷺ said:

"A woman was punished due to a cat she had imprisoned until it died, so she entered the Hellfire. She did not give it food or water while it was imprisoned, neither did she set it free to eat from the vermin of the earth." (Bukhārī, Muslim)

Sayyidunā Abū Hurairah ﵁ reported that the Prophet ﷺ said:

"A prostitute had once been forgiven. She passed by a dog panting near a well. Thirst had nearly killed the dog so she took off her sock, tied it to her veil and drew up some water. Allāh forgave her for that." (Bukhārī, Muslim)

Once a pious person saw Bāyazīd Bustāmi ﵀ in a dream and asked him how he had fared in front of Allāh ﷻ. He replied, "I have been granted forgiveness from Allāh ﷻ, not directly due to my good deeds but for showing kindness to a kitten. One dark night, I had gone out to find a kitten which was shivering due to the excessive cold. Upon seeing it in this misery, I took the kitten home and wrapped it up in a blanket and gave it some milk to drink. The kitten raised its paws in making du'ā for me and as a result, Allāh ﷻ forgave me."

إِنَّمَا يَنْهَاكُمُ اللَّهُ عَنِ الَّذِينَ قَاتَلُوكُمْ فِي الدِّينِ وَأَخْرَجُوكُم مِّن دِيَارِكُمْ وَظَاهَرُوا عَلَىٰ
إِخْرَاجِكُمْ أَن تَوَلَّوْهُمْ ۚ وَمَن يَتَوَلَّهُمْ فَأُولَٰئِكَ هُمُ الظَّالِمُونَ ۞

"Allāh forbids you from befriending only those (disbelievers) who fight you for (reason of your) religion, who drive you out of your homes and who assist (your enemies) in driving you out. Those (Muslims) who befriend them are certainly oppressors." (60:9)

The believers were forbidden from befriending and taking as allies those disbelievers who had shown them enmity and hatred due to Islām.

Sayyidunā Hātib ibn Abī Balta'ah رضي الله عنه thought by doing the polytheists a favour, i.e. delivering the letter to the polytheists warning them about the Prophet ﷺ marching out to Makkah, he felt that in exchange, they would protect his family and ensure that they came to no harm. What he failed to realise was that by exposing the plan of the Prophet ﷺ, he jeopardised the safety of all the believers because the disbelievers would stop at nothing to ensure the believers were exterminated, once and for all.

يَا أَيُّهَا الَّذِينَ آمَنُوا إِذَا جَاءَكُمُ الْمُؤْمِنَاتُ مُهَاجِرَاتٍ فَامْتَحِنُوهُنَّ ۖ اللَّهُ أَعْلَمُ بِإِيمَانِهِنَّ ۖ فَإِنْ
عَلِمْتُمُوهُنَّ مُؤْمِنَاتٍ فَلَا تَرْجِعُوهُنَّ إِلَى الْكُفَّارِ ۖ لَا هُنَّ حِلٌّ لَّهُمْ وَلَا هُمْ يَحِلُّونَ لَهُنَّ ۖ
وَآتُوهُم مَّا أَنفَقُوا ۚ وَلَا جُنَاحَ عَلَيْكُمْ أَن تَنكِحُوهُنَّ إِذَا آتَيْتُمُوهُنَّ أُجُورَهُنَّ ۚ وَلَا تُمْسِكُوا

بِعِصَمِ الْكَوَافِرِ وَاسْأَلُوا مَا أَنفَقْتُمْ وَلْيَسْأَلُوا مَا أَنفَقُوا ۚ ذَٰلِكُمْ حُكْمُ اللَّهِ ۖ يَحْكُمُ بَيْنَكُمْ ۚ وَاللَّهُ عَلِيمٌ حَكِيمٌ ۝

"O you who have īmān (faith)! When believing women come to you as immigrants, then examine them. Allāh best knows the condition of their īmān. If you determine that they are really believing women, then do not return them to the disbelievers. Neither are these women lawful as (wives) for the disbelieving men, nor are the disbelieving men lawful (as husbands) for these women. Return to them what they have spent. (Thereafter) there is no harm if you (Muslim men) marry these women when you give them their dowry. Do not stubbornly cling to your disbelieving wives. Ask for what (dowry) you have spent and let the disbelieving men ask (you) for what (dowries) they have spent. This is Allāh's command. Allāh decides between you and Allāh is All-Knowing, the Wise." (60:10)

In the peace treaty of Hudaybiyah the terms and conditions that were negotiated consisted of ten mandates. The pledge was biased in favour of the polytheists. One of the conditions was that if a person migrates from Makkah Mukkaramah to Madīnah Munawwarah, then they would have to be immediately returned back but if a person goes from Madīnah Munawwarah to Makkah Mukkaramah, they would not have to return them back. This was referring to the men. Regarding the women, they were not to be returned. They were only questioned, and the answers they gave were what the Prophet ﷺ used in deciding whether they were allowed to stay or be returned to Makkah Mukkaramah.

After the revelation of this verse, it was prohibited for a Muslim man or a Muslim woman to remain in a marriage with a disbeliever. The women who had migrated from Makkah leaving their disbelieving husbands were not allowed to be returned back to them after they had confessed their belief in the oneness of Allāh ﷻ. If a believer wished to marry any of the women whose marriage had become annulled as a result of their spouse's disbelief, they would have to pay the mahr (dowry) to their former husband, equivalent of what was given to the woman. Then the believing man could marry the believing woman after giving her a stipulated dowry (which would be a separate dowry than the one given to her former husband).

This verse was revealed after the peace treaty. For those women who wished to return back to Makkah Mukaramah in not accepting Islām, then the former husband had the right to demand back the dowry he had given to her during the marriage.

We should take things at face value, although there maybe times when what a person claims and what they carry out through their actions is contrary.

وَإِنْ فَاتَكُمْ شَيْءٌ مِّنْ أَزْوَاجِكُمْ إِلَى الْكُفَّارِ فَعَاقَبْتُمْ فَآتُوا الَّذِينَ ذَهَبَتْ أَزْوَاجُهُمْ مِّثْلَ مَا
أَنْفَقُوا ۚ وَاتَّقُوا اللَّهَ الَّذِي أَنْتُمْ بِهِ مُؤْمِنُونَ ۞

"If you (Muslim men) lose any of your wives to the disbelievers

and then you have your own back, then pay those who have lost their wives the equivalent of what they have spent. Fear Allāh in Whom you believe." (60:11)

Here, the situation became that the polytheists who had lost their wives as a result of them converting to Islām were compensated by the Muslims by having their dowry returned. However when the polytheists were expected to reciprocate on the same level by (returning the dowry back to the believing men when they married their former polytheist wives) they refused.

Allāh ﷻ is saying that if the polytheist men have not given the dowry to the believing men whose former polytheist wives they wished to marry, then the believers are to set aside the money in compensating the husband whose polytheist wife had left them. Allāh ﷻ revealed in this verse that this dowry should be retained and given to the believing men who had not received their fair share of mahr from the polytheist men who had then gone on to marry their former wives. To illustrate this, the following example is given:

A person has a wife or wives who are polytheists, so when the verse forbidding marriage between the believers and polytheists were revealed, he divorces his two wives. The men who would then marry his former wives would be expected to give the dowry to him. Now imagine that they refused to do so, but they also had a wife or wives who had accepted Islām and decided to marry a man from amongst the believers, the dowry which is required to be given to their polytheist husband should be retained and given to the person who lost out. This is how the system was based to ensure justice and fairness.

The word, 'Fa'āqabtum' (then your turn comes) which is used in this verse can have three meanings:

1) A person keeps the mahr instead of giving it to the polytheist man who has deprived a believing man of his fair share, with the intention of giving it to the believer who has been deprived of his share by the polytheist.

2) A person who is deprived of their share of mahr is given from the booty and spoils of war.

3) If a woman from the disbelievers comes to you as a Muslim and marries one of you, then compensate her non-Muslim ex in Makkah.

يَٰٓأَيُّهَا ٱلنَّبِيُّ إِذَا جَآءَكَ ٱلْمُؤْمِنَٰتُ يُبَايِعْنَكَ عَلَىٰٓ أَن لَّا يُشْرِكْنَ بِٱللَّهِ شَيْـًٔا وَلَا يَسْرِقْنَ وَلَا
يَزْنِينَ وَلَا يَقْتُلْنَ أَوْلَٰدَهُنَّ وَلَا يَأْتِينَ بِبُهْتَٰنٍ يَفْتَرِينَهُۥ بَيْنَ أَيْدِيهِنَّ وَأَرْجُلِهِنَّ وَلَا
يَعْصِينَكَ فِى مَعْرُوفٍ فَبَايِعْهُنَّ وَٱسْتَغْفِرْ لَهُنَّ ٱللَّهَ ۖ إِنَّ ٱللَّهَ غَفُورٌ رَّحِيمٌ ۝

"O Prophet! Accept the pledge of allegiance from the believing women and seek forgiveness from Allāh on their behalf when they come to you to pledge that they will not ascribe any partner to Allāh, that they will not steal, that they will not fornicate (or commit adultery), that they will not kill their children, that they

will not come forth with slander which they fabricate before their hands and legs and that they will not disobey you in any good. Indeed Allāh is Most Forgiving, Most Merciful." (60:12)

The pledge from the women was taken on the following six points:

1. That they would not commit shirk (ascribe partners with Allāh ﷻ).
2. They will not steal.
3. They will not commit zinā (fornication and adultery).
4. They will not kill their children.
5. They will not commit slander.
6. They will not disobey in matters of good.

Bay'ah refers to the oath of allegiance which the Prophet ﷺ took from both the men and women. There are different types of Bay'ah:

1) Bay'ah alal Islām – a person accepts Islām and pledges to remain steadfast upon their dīn.
2) Bay'ah alal khilāfah – a person takes a pledge of allegiance to the ruler. For example, when the Prophet ﷺ died, the people pledged their allegiance to Sayyidunā Abū Bakr رضي الله عنه.
3) Bay'ah alal jihād – when a pledge is taken to take up arms and fight in the path of Allāh ﷻ. For example, prior to the peace treaty of Hudaybiyah, Sayyidunā Uthmān رضي الله عنه went to do negotiations with the polytheists of Makkah. He was detained longer than anticipated and a rumour spread that the polytheists had killed Sayyidunā Uthmān رضي الله عنه. The 1400 Sahābah رضي الله عنهم took the

pledge of allegiance to fight in avenging the death of Sayyidunā Uthmān ﷺ.

4) Bay'ah alas sulūk – this is a pledge of allegiance for spiritual guidance. Sayyidunā Jarīr ibn Abdullāh Al-Bajali ﷺ says, "The Prophet ﷺ took this pledge from us that we will advise every Muslim regarding good things."

In another hadīth, it mentions that the Prophet ﷺ took bay'ah from the people of establishing salāh, giving zakāt and giving good counsel to every Muslim.

The purpose of taking bay'ah is so that a person is able to rectify themselves and carrying this out is fardh. The spiritual illnesses a person possesses in their hearts; they need to eradicate. If a person for example, has even an iota amount of pride in their hearts, then this person will be deprived of entering Paradise.

Sayyidunā Abdullāh ibn Mas'ūd ﷺ reported that the Prophet ﷺ said:

"No one who has the weight of a seed of arrogance in his heart will enter Paradise." Someone said, "But a man loves beautiful clothes and shoes." The Prophet said, "Verily Allāh is beautiful and He loves beauty. Arrogance means rejecting the truth and looking down on people." (Muslim)

In another hadīth, the Prophet ﷺ said:

"The one who prays and wants people to see them has committed shirk (ascribing partners to Allāh), the one who fasted and they want the people to know about their fasting has committed shirk. The one who gives sadaqah (charity) and wants people to know about their charity has committed shirk."

A person goes to the doctor for their physical ailments. Similarly, a spiritual guide; helps people eradicate their spiritual illnesses. When a person takes an oath of allegiance to a shaykh, a person agrees to abide by the rules taken in the pledge. The shaykh will also take into consideration a person's weaknesses, to tailor-make an individual programme suited to alleviating their spiritual ailments. For example, the shaykh may instruct a person to keep a beard, so he will include this alongside all the other points the person will pledge to abide by.

Another person may be neglecting their salāh, so the shaykh will make them pledge that they will perform their salāh. A woman for example, may not wear the hijāb, and they pledge with the shaykh that they will observe the hijāb.

During the time of the Prophet ﷺ, it was a common practice for women to get together and lament over the death of their loved ones. When the Prophet ﷺ was taking the pledge from the women, he stipulated the condition that the women would refrain from nawha (lamenting the dead). Sayyidah Hind bint Utbah ﷺ was also present during this time, and she immediately withdrew from taking the pledge saying that she could not go through with this. The Prophet asked her the reason, and she replied that she had already made a commitment to do nawha for a particular woman because she had done it for her relatives when they had passed away. He turned to her and said, "Only once." She agreed to this and then never carried out this act again.

Subhān-Allāh, the way the Prophet ﷺ assessed every situation on its individual merit. If the Prophet ﷺ had allowed her to go without taking her pledge, then she would have lost out greatly, and knowing that this was the only thing that was holding her back, he granted her exemption to do this so that she would then go on to take the pledge which would make her rectify her behaviour. This would not have occurred if he had refused to take her pledge; depriving her of all blessings.

Many a times, by allowing a person to work through their shortcomings, they are able to rise above it. For example, our Shaykh deals with many people suffering from the bad habit of smoking who come to him in seeking help. Instead of preventing it outright by saying that it is harām, he advises them the steps to take so that they could completely erase this bad habit without falling prey to going back to it. For example, when a person came to the Shaykh, smoking 20 cigarettes a day, he advised him to give up one cigarette a week until the habit was completely eradicated and many people had benefited in being able to give up in this way. Many a times, the situation has to be assessed, and measures have to be set to which is within the capability of the individual.

When a person is made to feel overburdened, then they may be reluctant to take the steps to make the necessary changes, feeling that it is beyond their capacity. Through breaking it down into small and more manageable steps, it enables the person to feel that it is within their reach, which may have felt unmanageable previously.

A baby has to learn how to sit down before learning how to crawl, and then they will develop the strength to hold them self up in standing upright; before learning how to walk. Similarly, a person who becomes steeped in sins is like a child that has fallen down. They need to be picked and helped back up, so that they can stand on their own two feet in rising up again.

If the injury is deep, then the healing can take weeks or even months but with patience and the correct level of support, the child recovers back to health. In the same way the shaykh alleviates the spiritual illness of the soul so that the soul is reinvigorated back to health; the person is then able to stand on their own two feet in combating the whisperings of their nafs (lower self) and Shaytān.

Just as a person cannot become a doctor by reading all the medical books in the world without associating themselves in the company of doctors, and learning from them; likewise, a person cannot rectify their own self without keeping the company of those who will show them the right way.

Once, a scholar came to Hakīm ul Ummah, Shaykh Ashraf Alī Thānwi ﷬ and said, "I am a scholar. I can study the books of tasawwuf (spirituality) and do my own spiritual remedy." Shaykh Ashraf Alī Thānwi ﷬ replied, "Tell me one thing; the word 'yuzakkīhim', is this faile lāzim (intransitive verb i.e. does not require an object) or faile muta'addī?"(transitive verb i.e. requires an object) The scholar immediately realised his mistake and said, "Hadhrat, this is it, I have understood." The word yuzakkīhim means to purify; i.e. a person cannot purify themself individually, they need a purifier, i.e. someone to guide them in seeking change.

Allāh ﷻ sent the Prophet ﷺ with the mission of accomplishing the following three things:

1) To recite the verses
2) To purify the people
3) To teach them the Book

In order to teach our children how to recite the Qur'ān, we send them to a supplementary school or a maktab where they are taught by a teacher. Every person needs to be taught, we cannot teach our selves. The Prophet ﷺ purified the Sahābah Kirām ﷵ; the Sahābah Kirām ﷵ sought to purify the Tābi'īn, the Tābi'īn purified the Tabi' Tābi'īn and this silsilah (chain) has continued into our time, and will continue up until the Day of Judgement.

﴿يَٰٓأَيُّهَا ٱلَّذِينَ ءَامَنُوا۟ ٱتَّقُوا۟ ٱللَّهَ وَكُونُوا۟ مَعَ ٱلصَّٰدِقِينَ﴾

"O you have īmān! fear Allāh and stay with the truthful." (9:119)

Nowadays, many people use the excuse, "I can't find any shaykh," or, "I can't find any true person to guide me." This ruling is until the Day of Judgement, so there will always be people true to their faith in this world. There may be fewer righteous people; we may not have Imām Rāzi, Shaykh Ashraf Alī Thānwi, Maulāna Qāsim Nānotwī or other scholars of their calibre, but there will always be scholars to guide us.

﴿أَن لَّا يُشْرِكْنَ بِٱللَّهِ شَيْـًٔا﴾

"They will not ascribe any partner to Allāh ." (60:12)

The first quality Allāh mentions is to abstain from committing shirk. Allāh says that even if the prophets committed shirk, their deeds would be nullified:

﴿وَلَقَدْ أُوحِىَ إِلَيْكَ وَإِلَى ٱلَّذِينَ مِن قَبْلِكَ لَئِنْ أَشْرَكْتَ لَيَحْبَطَنَّ عَمَلُكَ وَلَتَكُونَنَّ مِنَ ٱلْخَٰسِرِينَ﴾

"Indeed We have sent revelation to you (O Prophet) and to those (prophets) before you (stating), 'If you commit shirk, your (good) deeds will certainly be wasted and you will definitely become of the losers." (39:65)

In another verse Allāh ﷻ says:

وَزَكَرِيَّا وَيَحْيَىٰ وَعِيسَىٰ وَإِلْيَاسَ ۖ كُلٌّ مِّنَ الصَّالِحِينَ ﴿٨٥﴾ وَإِسْمَاعِيلَ وَالْيَسَعَ وَيُونُسَ
وَلُوطًا ۚ وَكُلًّا فَضَّلْنَا عَلَى الْعَالَمِينَ ﴿٨٦﴾ وَمِنْ آبَائِهِمْ وَذُرِّيَّاتِهِمْ وَإِخْوَانِهِمْ ۖ وَاجْتَبَيْنَاهُمْ
وَهَدَيْنَاهُمْ إِلَىٰ صِرَاطٍ مُّسْتَقِيمٍ ﴿٨٧﴾ ذَٰلِكَ هُدَى اللَّهِ يَهْدِي بِهِ مَن يَشَاءُ مِنْ عِبَادِهِ ۚ وَلَوْ
أَشْرَكُوا لَحَبِطَ عَنْهُم مَّا كَانُوا يَعْمَلُونَ ﴿٨٨﴾

"And Zakariyyā, Yahyā, Īsā and Ilyās, all of whom were from the righteous. And Ismā'īl, Yasa, Yūnus and Lūt. Each of them We favoured above the (people of the) universe. And from their forefathers, progeny and brothers. We chose them and guided them to the straight path. This is Allāh's guidance by which He guides whom He wills from His bondsmen. If they commit shirk, then all their actions will be destroyed." (6: 85-88)

قَدْ أَفْلَحَ مَن زَكَّاهَا ﴿٩﴾ وَقَدْ خَابَ مَن دَسَّاهَا ﴿١٠﴾

"Undoubtedly the one who purified has succeeded and the one who soiled it has certainly failed." (91: 9-10)

﴿ وَلَا يَسْرِقْنَ ﴾

"That they will not steal." (60:12)

The second condition was that they would refrain from stealing. At the time when Sayyidah Hind رضي الله عنها was about to take her pledge, when she heard this condition, Sayyidah Hind رضي الله عنها immediately removed her hand saying, "My husband Abū Sufyān is a miserly person and many a times, I have had to take money from him without his knowledge." Abū Sufyān ﷺ was in the Majlis and upon hearing this said, "I have forgiven you, continue taking the bay'ah."

﴿ وَلَا يَزْنِينَ ﴾

"They will not fornicate (or commit adultery)." (60:12)

The word zinā includes both fornication and adultery.

﴿ وَلَا يَقْتُلْنَ أَوْلَادَهُنَّ ﴾

"That they will not kill their children." (60:12)

When the Prophet ﷺ instructed this condition as part of the pledge, one woman stood up and said, "It was not us who do this, it was the men who committed this act."

Allāh ﷻ says regarding their actions:

﴿ يَتَوَارَىٰ مِنَ الْقَوْمِ مِن سُوءِ مَا بُشِّرَ بِهِ ۚ أَيُمْسِكُهُ عَلَىٰ هُونٍ أَمْ يَدُسُّهُ فِي التُّرَابِ ۗ أَلَا سَاءَ مَا يَحْكُمُونَ ﴾

"When any of them is given the good news of a daughter, his face darkens and he suppresses his fury. He hides from the people because of the terrible news that he received. Must he keep her with disgrace or bury her in the sand. Evil indeed is the decision that they make!" (16:59)

Some of the women used to have illicit affairs and when they would give birth, they would ascribe the child to their husband when in fact it was the child of the man whom they had engaged in an extra-marital relationship with.

﴿وَلَا يَأْتِينَ بِبُهْتَانٍ يَفْتَرِينَهُۥ بَيْنَ أَيْدِيهِنَّ وَأَرْجُلِهِنَّ﴾

"That they will not come forth with slander which they fabricate before their hands and legs." (60:12)

They would lie through their teeth whilst their limbs were witness to this act, and on the Day of Judgement, Allāh ﷻ will seal their mouths and their hands and feet will give witness:

﴿ٱلْيَوْمَ نَخْتِمُ عَلَىٰٓ أَفْوَٰهِهِمْ وَتُكَلِّمُنَآ أَيْدِيهِمْ وَتَشْهَدُ أَرْجُلُهُم بِمَا كَانُوا۟ يَكْسِبُونَ﴾

"On this day We shall seal their mouths. Their hands will speak to Us and their legs will testify to what they earned." (36:65)

﴿وَلَا يَعْصِينَكَ فِى مَعْرُوفٍ﴾

"And that they will not disobey you in any good." (60:12)

This highlights the importance of obeying the Prophet ﷺ even though it might have gone against a person's personal inclinations or preferences.

﴿إِنَّ ٱللَّهَ غَفُورٌ رَّحِيمٌ﴾

"Indeed Allāh is Most Forgiving, Most Merciful." (60:12)

After a person takes bay'ah, the du'ā for istighfār (seeking forgiveness) is made.

Sayyidunā Jarīr ibn Abdullāh Al-Bajali رضي الله عنه *Re-Negotiates in Giving Double*

Sayyidunā Jarīr ibn Abdullāh Al-Bajali رضي الله عنه took the bay'ah pledging that he would establish salāh, pay zakāt and give good counsel to every Muslim. Once Sayyidunā Jarīr رضي الله عنه sent his servant to purchase a horse. Upon the servant returning back home he asked him, "How much did you pay for the horse?"

The servant replied, "400 dirhams." Sayyidunā Jarīr رضي الله عنه immediately instructed his servant to take him to the place from where he had purchased the horse. He found the seller and said to him, "My servant purchased this horse from you and I would like to re-negotiate the price."

The man replied that the deal had been done and there was nothing left to negotiate. Sayyidunā Jarīr رضي الله عنه explained further, "Let me clarify this matter. I want to give you 500 dirhams for the horse." The man became shocked and said, "500? Of course, why not!" Sayyidunā Jarīr رضي الله عنه replied, "I'll give you 600 dirhams." The man became even more ecstatic to which Sayyidunā Jarīr رضي الله عنه said, "I will give you 700 dirhams... 800 dirhams?" The man gladly accepted. The money was given to the seller and then Sayyidunā Jarīr ﷺ headed off home.

On the way back, he met a friend who asked how much he had purchased the horse for. When he replied that he had purchased the horse for 800 dirhams, his friend said that he had been fooled into paying too much, explaining that he had also passed by the horse, and the man had offered to sell it to him for 400 dirhams. Sayyidunā Jarīr ﷺ replied that the seller had also offered him the same price but he had felt that the seller had underestimated the price, and as he had pledged to the Prophet ﷺ that he would give sincere counsel to the Muslims, he could not accept a horse which he had not paid the adequate price for.

The commitment the Sahābah Kirām ﷺ showed in fulfilling their pledges leaves us astonished and filled with wonder. Another group of Sahābah Kirām ﷺ had pledged that they would not ask any favours from others to the extent that if they had mounted their camels and something had fallen on the ground, which could have easily been picked up and given to them by a person standing nearby, they refrained from asking. They felt that because they had taken the pledge to refrain from asking favours from others, this would amount to asking for a favour, so they would get down themselves to pick it up.

Sayyidunā Abdullāh ibn Amr ibn Al-Ās's ﷺ Dedication

Sayyidunā Abdullāh ibn Amr ibn Al-Ās ﷺ used to complete the recitation of the entire Qur'ān in his Tahajjud Salāh at night, followed by fasting during the daylight hours. The Prophet ﷺ felt that this practice was excessive for him and he recommended for him to recite one juz everyday, saying that in this way he would be able to complete one khatm (completion) every month. Sayyidunā Abdullāh ibn Amr ﷺ insisted that he would be able to recite more, to which the Prophet ﷺ increased this to three juz a day. He further insisted to which the Prophet ﷺ replied that he should recite one manzil (one-seventh of the Qur'ān) daily.

Due to the fact that this was the amount he had agreed upon with the Prophet ﷺ before he (Prophet ﷺ) passed away, he continued on with this practice. He lived well into his nineties, but even then, he remained firm on this practice. This was the last agreement he had made with the Prophet ﷺ before he passed away. He felt that if he did not keep up this practice then he would have failed in keeping his word.

In one piece of advice, the Prophet ﷺ advised Sayyidunā Abdullāh ibn Umar ﷺ not to be like the person who would stand up in the night time prayer and then ended up leaving it. This refers to remaining steadfast when we commit ourselves to carrying out good deeds.

Sayyidah Ā'ishah ﷺ narrates that the Prophet ﷺ was asked, *"What deeds are loved most by Allāh?" He said, "The most regular constant deeds even though they may be few." He added, 'Don't take upon yourselves except the deeds which are within your ability."* (Bukhārī)

يَٰٓأَيُّهَا ٱلَّذِينَ ءَامَنُوا۟ لَا تَتَوَلَّوْا۟ قَوْمًا غَضِبَ ٱللَّهُ عَلَيْهِمْ قَدْ يَئِسُوا۟ مِنَ ٱلْءَاخِرَةِ كَمَا يَئِسَ ٱلْكُفَّارُ مِنْ أَصْحَٰبِ ٱلْقُبُورِ ۝

"O you who have īmān (faith)! Do not befriend a nation with whom Allāh is angry and who have lost hope in the Ākhirah (Hereafter) just as the disbelievers in the graves have lost hope." (60:13)

This refers to the disbelievers. During the time of the Prophet ﷺ, there were those who showed outright enmity and hatred for Islām, despite knowing in their hearts that this was the truth. Their arrogance and pride would not allow them to accept the message despite witnessing so many signs and evidence. In summarising the message in this sūrah; those who show friendship and love; a person should reciprocate this back, but those who behave with enmity, a person must remain cautious in their dealings with them.

May Allāh ﷻ allow us to deal with people in spreading the love and compassion that Islām truly stands for. Āmīn.

English Translation of

سورة الممتحنة

Sūrah 60 Al Mumtahinah (The Examined One)

(Madani | 13 Verses)

O you who have īmān (faith)! Do not take My enemy and your enemy as friends, offering your friendship to them when they reject the truth that has come to you. They have driven out the Messenger and yourselves because you believe in Allāh as your Lord. If you emerge to strive in My path and to seek My pleasure (you would not befriend the disbelievers). You secretly show friendship to them when I am Aware of what you conceal and what you reveal. The one who does this from among you has certainly strayed from the straight path.	1	يَٰٓأَيُّهَا ٱلَّذِينَ ءَامَنُوا۟ لَا تَتَّخِذُوا۟ عَدُوِّى وَعَدُوَّكُمْ أَوْلِيَآءَ تُلْقُونَ إِلَيْهِم بِٱلْمَوَدَّةِ وَقَدْ كَفَرُوا۟ بِمَا جَآءَكُم مِّنَ ٱلْحَقِّ يُخْرِجُونَ ٱلرَّسُولَ وَإِيَّاكُمْ ۙ أَن تُؤْمِنُوا۟ بِٱللَّهِ رَبِّكُمْ إِن كُنتُمْ خَرَجْتُمْ جِهَٰدًا فِى سَبِيلِى وَٱبْتِغَآءَ مَرْضَاتِى ۚ تُسِرُّونَ إِلَيْهِم بِٱلْمَوَدَّةِ وَأَنَا۠ أَعْلَمُ بِمَآ أَخْفَيْتُمْ وَمَآ أَعْلَنتُمْ ۚ وَمَن يَفْعَلْهُ مِنكُمْ فَقَدْ ضَلَّ سَوَآءَ ٱلسَّبِيلِ ۝
If they (the disbelievers) find you they will be enemies to you and extend their tongues and hands towards you with evil intent. They wish that you were disbelievers (like them).	2	إِن يَثْقَفُوكُمْ يَكُونُوا۟ لَكُمْ أَعْدَآءً وَيَبْسُطُوٓا۟ إِلَيْكُمْ أَيْدِيَهُمْ وَأَلْسِنَتَهُم بِٱلسُّوٓءِ وَوَدُّوا۟ لَوْ تَكْفُرُونَ ۝
Neither your relatives nor your children will help you on the Day	3	لَن تَنفَعَكُمْ أَرْحَامُكُمْ وَلَآ

of Judgement. You will be separated. Allāh is Watchful over what you do.		أَوْلَادُكُمْ ۚ يَوْمَ الْقِيٰمَةِ ۚ يَفْصِلُ بَيْنَكُمْ ۗ وَاللّٰهُ بِمَا تَعْمَلُوْنَ بَصِيْرٌ ۝
There was certainly an excellent example for you in Ibrāhīm and those who followed him when they said to their people, "We absolve ourselves from you and from that which you worship apart from Allāh. We reject you (your beliefs). Enmity and hatred have surfaced between yourselves and us forever until you believe in one Allāh." Except for the statement of Ibrāhīm to his father when he said, "I shall definitely pray to Allāh for your forgiveness. I have no power to do anything for you against (the punishment of) Allāh. O our Lord! In You do we trust, to You do we turn and to You shall we return."	4	قَدْ كَانَتْ لَكُمْ أُسْوَةٌ حَسَنَةٌ فِيْٓ إِبْرٰهِيْمَ وَالَّذِيْنَ مَعَهٗ ۚ إِذْ قَالُوْا لِقَوْمِهِمْ إِنَّا بُرَءٰٓؤُا مِنْكُمْ وَمِمَّا تَعْبُدُوْنَ مِنْ دُوْنِ اللّٰهِ ۫ كَفَرْنَا بِكُمْ وَبَدَا بَيْنَنَا وَبَيْنَكُمُ الْعَدَاوَةُ وَالْبَغْضَآءُ أَبَدًا حَتّٰى تُؤْمِنُوْا بِاللّٰهِ وَحْدَهٗٓ إِلَّا قَوْلَ إِبْرٰهِيْمَ لِأَبِيْهِ لَأَسْتَغْفِرَنَّ لَكَ وَمَآ أَمْلِكُ لَكَ مِنَ اللّٰهِ مِنْ شَيْءٍ ۚ رَبَّنَا عَلَيْكَ تَوَكَّلْنَا وَإِلَيْكَ أَنَبْنَا وَإِلَيْكَ الْمَصِيْرُ ۝
O our Lord! Do not make us a test for the disbelievers and forgive (us). O our Lord, Indeed	5	رَبَّنَا لَا تَجْعَلْنَا فِتْنَةً لِّلَّذِيْنَ كَفَرُوْا وَاغْفِرْ لَنَا رَبَّنَا ۚ إِنَّكَ أَنْتَ الْعَزِيْزُ

You are the Mighty, the Wise.		الْحَكِيْمُ ۞
There was certainly an excellent example in them for those of you who believe in Allāh and the Last Day. As for him who turns away, Allāh certainly is Independent, Most worthy of Praise.	6	لَقَدْ كَانَ لَكُمْ فِيْهِمْ أُسْوَةٌ حَسَنَةٌ لِّمَنْ كَانَ يَرْجُوا اللّٰهَ وَالْيَوْمَ الْاٰخِرَ ؕ وَمَنْ يَّتَوَلَّ فَإِنَّ اللّٰهَ هُوَ الْغَنِيُّ الْحَمِيْدُ ۞
Allāh shall soon create love between you and those who are your enemies. Allāh is Most Capable and Allāh is Most Forgiving, Most Merciful.	7	عَسَى اللّٰهُ أَنْ يَّجْعَلَ بَيْنَكُمْ وَبَيْنَ الَّذِيْنَ عَادَيْتُمْ مِّنْهُمْ مَّوَدَّةً ؕ وَاللّٰهُ قَدِيْرٌ ؕ وَاللّٰهُ غَفُوْرٌ رَّحِيْمٌ ۞
Allāh does not forbid you from behaving cordially and justly towards those who do not fight you for (reason of your) religion and who do not drive you out from your homes. Verily Allāh loves those who are just.	8	لَا يَنْهٰكُمُ اللّٰهُ عَنِ الَّذِيْنَ لَمْ يُقَاتِلُوْكُمْ فِي الدِّيْنِ وَلَمْ يُخْرِجُوْكُمْ مِّنْ دِيَارِكُمْ أَنْ تَبَرُّوْهُمْ وَتُقْسِطُوْٓا إِلَيْهِمْ ؕ إِنَّ اللّٰهَ يُحِبُّ الْمُقْسِطِيْنَ ۞
Allāh forbids you from befriending only those (disbelievers) who fight you for (reason of your) religion, who	9	إِنَّمَا يَنْهٰكُمُ اللّٰهُ عَنِ الَّذِيْنَ قٰتَلُوْكُمْ فِي الدِّيْنِ وَأَخْرَجُوْكُمْ مِّنْ دِيَارِكُمْ وَظٰهَرُوْا عَلٰٓى إِخْرَاجِكُمْ أَنْ

drive you out of your homes and who assist (your enemies) in driving you out. Those (Muslims) who befriend them are certainly oppressors.	9	تَوَلَّوْهُمْ ۚ وَمَنْ يَتَوَلَّهُمْ فَأُولَٰئِكَ هُمُ الظَّالِمُونَ ۝
O you who have īmān (faith)! When believing women come to you as immigrants, then examine them. Allāh best knows the condition of their īmān. If you determine that they are really believing women, then do not return them to the disbelievers. Neither are these women lawful as (wives) for the disbelieving men, nor are the disbelieving men lawful (as husbands) for these women. Return to them what they have spent. (Thereafter) there is no harm if you (Muslim men) marry these women when you give them their dowries. Do not stubbornly cling to your disbelieving wives. Ask for what (dowries) you have spent and let the disbelieving men ask	10	يَا أَيُّهَا الَّذِينَ آمَنُوا إِذَا جَاءَكُمُ الْمُؤْمِنَاتُ مُهَاجِرَاتٍ فَامْتَحِنُوهُنَّ ۖ اللَّهُ أَعْلَمُ بِإِيمَانِهِنَّ ۖ فَإِنْ عَلِمْتُمُوهُنَّ مُؤْمِنَاتٍ فَلَا تَرْجِعُوهُنَّ إِلَى الْكُفَّارِ ۖ لَا هُنَّ حِلٌّ لَهُمْ وَلَا هُمْ يَحِلُّونَ لَهُنَّ ۖ وَآتُوهُمْ مَا أَنْفَقُوا ۚ وَلَا جُنَاحَ عَلَيْكُمْ أَنْ تَنْكِحُوهُنَّ إِذَا آتَيْتُمُوهُنَّ أُجُورَهُنَّ ۚ وَلَا تُمْسِكُوا بِعِصَمِ الْكَوَافِرِ وَاسْأَلُوا مَا أَنْفَقْتُمْ وَلْيَسْأَلُوا مَا أَنْفَقُوا ۚ ذَٰلِكُمْ حُكْمُ اللَّهِ ۖ يَحْكُمُ بَيْنَكُمْ ۚ وَاللَّهُ عَلِيمٌ حَكِيمٌ ۝

(you) for what (dowries) they have spent. This is Allāh's command. Allāh decides between you and Allāh is All-Knowing, the Wise.		
If you (Muslim men) lose any of your wives to the disbelievers and then you have your own back, then pay those who have lost their wives the equivalent of what they have spent. Fear Allāh in Whom you believe.	11	وَإِن فَاتَكُمْ شَيْءٌ مِّنْ أَزْوَاجِكُمْ إِلَى الْكُفَّارِ فَعَاقَبْتُمْ فَآتُوا الَّذِينَ ذَهَبَتْ أَزْوَاجُهُم مِّثْلَ مَا أَنفَقُوا ۚ وَاتَّقُوا اللَّهَ الَّذِي أَنتُم بِهِ مُؤْمِنُونَ ۝
O Prophet! Accept the pledge of allegiance from the believing women and seek forgiveness from Allāh on their behalf when they come to you to pledge that they will not ascribe any partner to Allāh , that they will not steal, that they will not fornicate (or commit adultery), that they will not kill their children, that they will not come forth with slander which they fabricate before their hands and legs and that they will	12	يَا أَيُّهَا النَّبِيُّ إِذَا جَاءَكَ الْمُؤْمِنَاتُ يُبَايِعْنَكَ عَلَىٰ أَن لَّا يُشْرِكْنَ بِاللَّهِ شَيْئًا وَلَا يَسْرِقْنَ وَلَا يَزْنِينَ وَلَا يَقْتُلْنَ أَوْلَادَهُنَّ وَلَا يَأْتِينَ بِبُهْتَانٍ يَفْتَرِينَهُ بَيْنَ أَيْدِيهِنَّ وَأَرْجُلِهِنَّ وَلَا يَعْصِينَكَ فِي مَعْرُوفٍ فَبَايِعْهُنَّ وَاسْتَغْفِرْ لَهُنَّ اللَّهَ ۚ إِنَّ اللَّهَ غَفُورٌ رَّحِيمٌ ۝

not disobey you in any good. Indeed Allāh is Most Forgiving, Most Merciful.		
O you who have īmān (faith)! Do not befriend a nation with whom Allāh is angry and who have lost hope in the Ākhirah (Hereafter) just as the disbelievers in the graves have lost hope.	13	يَٰٓأَيُّهَا ٱلَّذِينَ ءَامَنُوا۟ لَا تَتَوَلَّوْا۟ قَوْمًا غَضِبَ ٱللَّهُ عَلَيْهِمْ قَدْ يَئِسُوا۟ مِنَ ٱلْءَاخِرَةِ كَمَا يَئِسَ ٱلْكُفَّارُ مِنْ أَصْحَٰبِ ٱلْقُبُورِ ۝

Quranic Wonders

The science of Tafsīr in itself is very vast, hence the compilation of these specific verses provides the reader with a simple and brief commentary. It is aimed to equip the reader with a small glimpse of the profound beauty of the Holy Qur'ān so that they can gain the passion to study further in depth. It is hoped that this will become a means of encouragement to increase the zeal and enthusiasm to recite and inculcate the teachings of the Holy Qur'ān into our daily lives. **UK RRP:£5:00**

Protection in the Grave
Sūrah Al-Mulk encapsulates the purpose of our creation - that we were created to live a life of obedience to our Lord and Creator. This can only be made to manifest through our good deeds which we perform solely for the sake of Allāh ﷻ, in order to seek His pleasure. The Holy Prophet ﷺ told his Ummah to recite this Sūrah every night and learn this Sūrah by heart. The importance of this Sūrah is stressed due to the fact that the Holy Prophet ﷺ never slept until he had finished reciting this Sūrah. **UK RRP:£4:00**

Protection from Black Magic
These last ten Sūrahs are not only distinct in their meanings and message which will be discussed in this book, but also the fact that every Muslim should have these Sūrahs committed to memory as a minimum requirement in seeking refuge in Allāh ﷻ from all harm and evil, and every imperfection as well as seeking solace and peace in understanding His might and attributes. **UK RRP:£5:00**

Nurturing Children in Islam
Bringing up children has never been an easy duty. The challenges do not get easier as they get older either. Our emotions and other priorities sometimes hinder in nurturing our children, and as such, we fail to assist our children in reaching their potential by continually stumbling over our own perception of what we consider as ideal children. Our duty to our children is not without accountability. Our neglect and lack of interest in our children will be held to task. **UK RRP:£5:00**

Best of Stories

Sūrah Yūsuf is more than just a story of one of our beloved Prophets ﷺ, there is much wisdom and lessons to be learnt and understood. All the knowledge comes from our honourable Shaykh, inspiration and Ustādh, Shaykh Mufti Saiful Islām Sāhib. May Allāh ﷻ shower Mufti Sāhib with mercy and accept the day in, day out effort he carries out in the work of Dīn. **UK RRP:£4:00**

Call of Nuh

For 950 years, Sayyidunā Nūh ﷺ persevered night and day in continuous succession in preaching the message; unwavering and relentless in his mission. Not once did he feel that his calling was in vain. He stood firm and resolute in continuing with the mission that he was sent with, in proclaiming the message of the oneness of Allāh ﷻ; year after year, decade upon decade, century after century, but this failed to convince the people of the truth. **UK RRP:£4:00**

A Glimpse of Paradise

Time is the true wealth we have at our disposal though it cannot be amassed. The only way we can utilise it to our advantage is when we do righteous deeds and actions; for this will act in our favour in the Ākhirah (Hereafter). These moments will be preserved in exchange for moments of greater happiness and bliss in the next life. Therefore, we need to perform righteous deeds and actions in the short duration of time we have at our disposal in this temporary worldly life.

UK RRP:£4:00

Six Qualities of a Believer

Respected readers, do you want to be successful in this life and the Hereafter? The fact that you have prompted yourself to pick up this book and read, is an indication that the answer is *yes*. Or perhaps, you were not aware of the contents and purpose of this book and hence, eternal success wasn't the first thing on your mind. Nonetheless, it is easy to turn your attention towards this objective right now. **UK RRP:£2:00**

Ready for Judgement Day?
For those that doubt the Day of Resurrection, Allāh ﷻ is reaffirming that there is no scope for uncertainty; this day is indisputable and will surely occur. The day when the truth will be laid out bare and everything will be exposed, there will be no place to flee or escape to. Regretting that day will be of no avail; excuses will fail to safeguard or shelter a person from breaking free and escaping judgement. **UK RRP:£4:00**

Flee Towards Allāh ﷻ
Sūrah Al-Ma'ārij begins by addressing the disbelievers who used to mock the Holy Prophet ﷺ about the Day of Judgement. In this Surah, Allāh ﷻ severely reproaches those who deny it assuming that there is only one life; the life of this world. The Sūrah manifests its horrors and catastrophic scenes that the entire creation shall witness on that very day. Mankind will then realise that on this horrific day, they will be judged by their own actions. **UK RRP:£4:00**

Lanterns of Knowledge
Once the commentary of Kitābul 'Ilm in Bukhāri was completed, we realised that this chapter is an entire topic in itself due to its fascinating and insightful perspective on knowledge. When compiling this commentary, there were many beautiful reminders as well as points of guidance for everyone's personal life as well as their lifelong quest for knowledge. Therefore, the commentary of this chapter alone would be beneficial for all seekers of knowledge and the idea of publishing it as a separate book came to mind. **UK RRP:£10:00**

TIME IS RUNNING OUT
As the title suggests, as each day passes, we come closer to our death. Life is too short to be treated as an amusement and for the fulfillment of one's lust. The Day of Judgement is inevitable where we all must one day stand in front of the Lord of the Worlds to give an account of our deeds. These six Sūrahs explain the horrors and terrifying moments of Judgement Day and the inevitable standing before the Lord. We must therefore prepare for the Hereafter by realizing our purpose in life; to worship Allāh ﷻ Alone and reduce our worldly expectations. **UK RRP:£4:00**

Living Islām in Modern Times
This book is a compilation of various articles written by Shaykh Dr. Rafāqat Rashīd Sāhib in the popular Al-Mu'min Magazine. Considering the great benefit these articles will bring to the Ummah, Mufti Saiful Islām Sāhib decided to edit and transform them into a book format, making the content easily accessible for readers.

UK RRP:£4:00

A CLEAR VICTORY
This book "A Clear Victory" is an enlightening commentary of Sūrah Al-Fath. It is cited in Sahīh Al-Bukhāri regarding the virtue of this Sūrah that Sayyidunā Umar Ibn Al-Khattāb ﷺ reported that the Messenger of Allāh ﷺ said: "This night a Sūrah was sent down to me that is more beloved to me than all what the sun shines over," then he read, "*We have indeed accorded a triumph to you, a manifest triumph, indeed*". **UK RRP:£5:00**

A DAY WITH THE PROPHET ﷺ
This book is a collection of the daily Prophetic Sunnats - practices and habits - a guide for us all to follow. The objective behind this book is to instil the love for the Prophet ﷺ by encouraging our readers to implement his Sunnats into their daily lives. The daily Sunnats range from worship to general social and personal etiquettes and conduct. Each habit relative to a specific Sunnah is referenced from a hadīth. **UK RRP:£5:00**

BEWARE OF HYPOCRISY
The Munāfiqūn (hypocrites) were a group of people who did not have the courage to openly oppose the holy Prophet ﷺ feeling that it would be unfavourable in their favour if they wished to find a way of overpowering the Muslims. Sūrah Munāfiqūn explains the true traits of the hypocrites during the time of the Prophet ﷺ, warning the believers to take precaution from their treacherous behaviours. **UK RRP:£3:00**

DIVORCE IN ISLAM

The proper functioning of human race depends on the proper maintenance of marital relationship. Islām has focused attention on family issues most exhaustively. By a careful analysis of the holy Qur᾿ān, we notice that commercial contracts like sale, partnership, hiring and so on are though among the most important socio-economic matters, the holy Qur᾿ān has restricted itself to setting down their basic principles, and the bye-laws are rarely ever touched upon. **UK RRP:£4:00**

MIND YOUR OWN BUSINESS

This book is a gateway towards understanding how to live a sharī'ah-compliant life in business. By adhering to these guidelines, you are sure to attract the blessings of Allāh ﷻ in this world and the Hereafter, and live a life of true happiness and contentment. The lessons included in it are not just to be read, but to be lived. And that must start today. Not tomorrow. Not next year. Today.
UK RRP:£4:00

MISERY BEYOND DEATH

One of the aspects which differentiates a Muslim from a non-Muslim is the belief in the Ākhirah (Hereafter). Muslims believe that they will be held accountable for wrongdoings and rewarded for good. Sūrah Mursalāt discusses in detail the catastrophic scenes on the Day of Judgement, when the record of deeds of each and every individual will be laid open in front of them. The shock and horror of that day will be extraordinary. **UK RRP:£4:00**

A MUSLIM'S GUIDE TO PANDEMICS

A person will face many different challenges throughout their life. However, the beauty of Islām lies in the mere fact that it has all the answers to every possible situation. A Muslim may be struggling to cope, yet the holy Qur'ān and ahādīth are filled with antidotes to these struggles. As Muslims, we are encouraged to view our calamities as blessings. More so, it is an opportunity for us to turn to Allāh ﷻ with a sincere heart and strengthen our īmān (faith).
UK RRP:£4:00

WATCH YOUR CHARACTER

In Sūrah Qalam, Allāh ﷻ defended the holy Prophet ﷺ of his elevated rank as being raised to a position of great spiritual dignity, ingrained in the very fundamental structure of his being, which moulded him with a disposition and temperament far greater than that of any being to have ever existed. Sūrah Qalam also teaches us to inculcate good habits and shun aside all bad habits. **UK RRP:£5:00**

THE WORLD OF JINNS

Allāh ﷻ created the Jinns which also reside on the Earth. Just as there are Muslims and non-Muslims in the human beings, so too, there are Muslims and non-Muslims amongst the Jinns. Sūrah Jinn is full of references to the holy Qur'ān and hadīth, exploring and providing insight into this creation which we have little knowledge about. We will find much theories on this creation which are only speculative and baseless. **UK RRP:£4:00**

ACTIONS SPEAK LOUDER THAN WORDS

Sūrah As-Saff teaches us some fundamental ways of how to live our lives as believers and not be deceived by the materialistic things of this worldly life. In order to achieve this, we can take inspiration by looking at the lives of the Sahābah ﷺ and our pious predecessors. They were firm in acting upon the things they would preach. We need to keep in mind that when we remain true to our pledge, then Allāh ﷻ will allow us to remain dominant over everyone else. **UK RRP:£3:00**